THE HERO TWINS

AGAINST THE LORDS OF DEATH

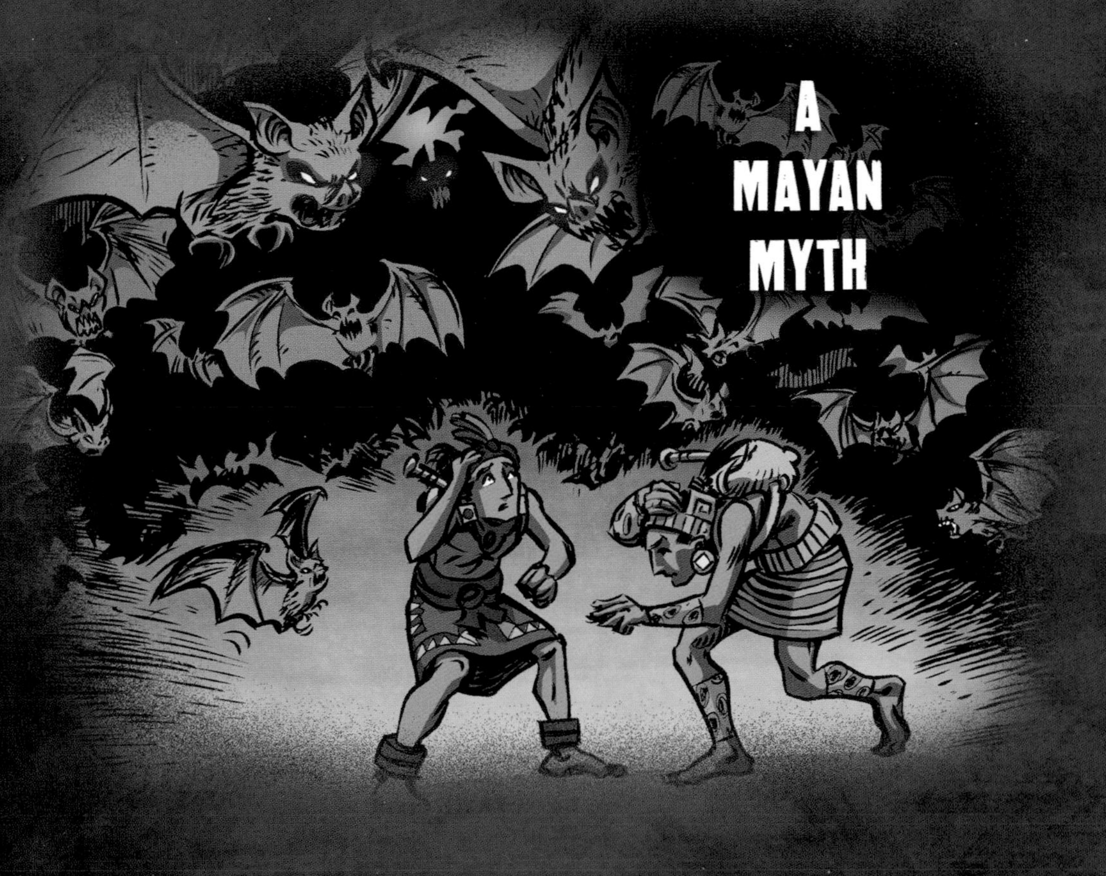

A MAYAN MYTH

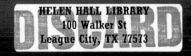

STORY BY
DAN JOLLEY
PENCILS AND INKS BY
DAVID WITT

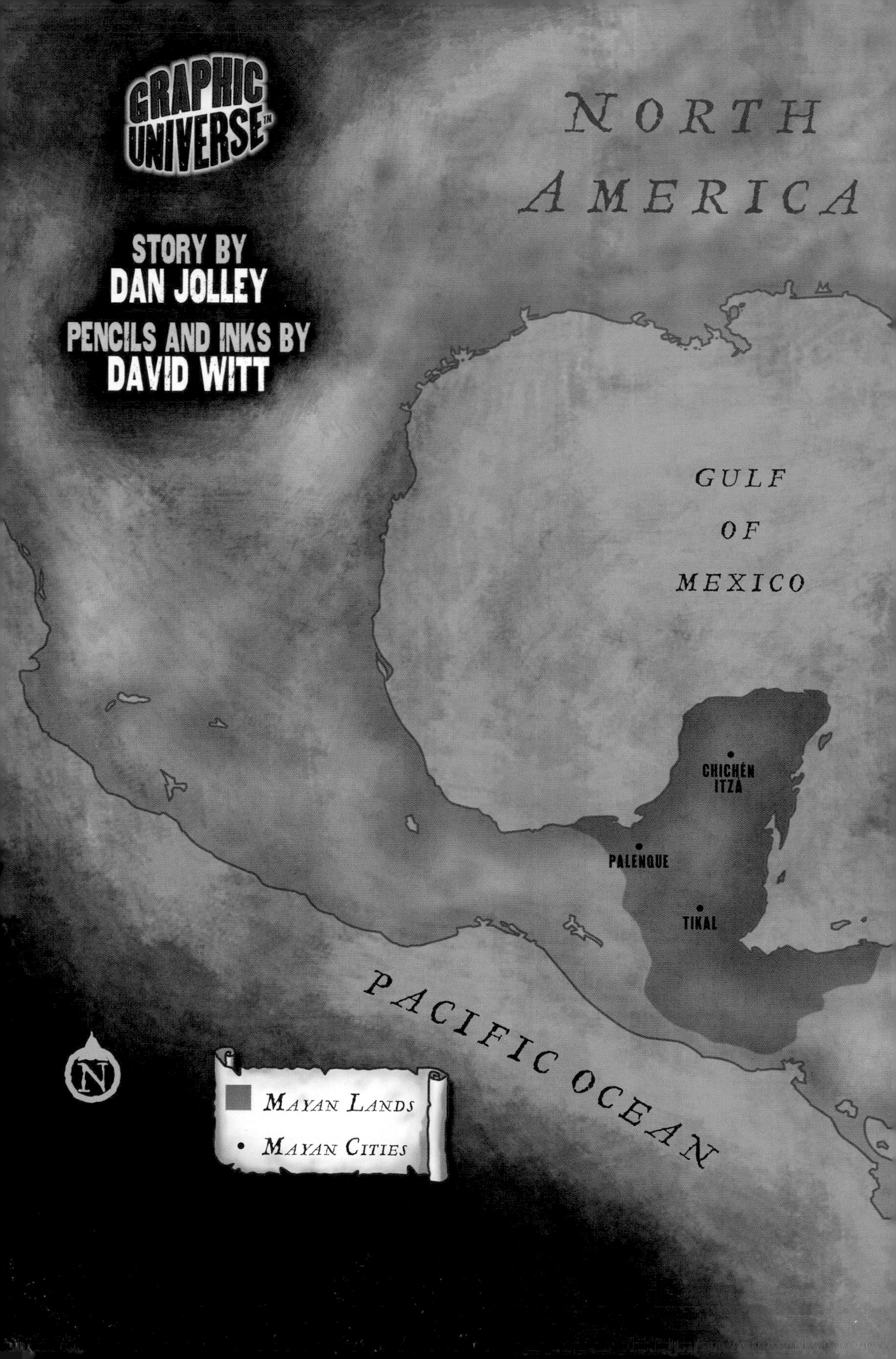
NORTH AMERICA
GULF OF MEXICO
CHICHÉN ITZÁ
PALENQUE
TIKAL
PACIFIC OCEAN
N
MAYAN LANDS
MAYAN CITIES

THE HERO TWINS

AGAINST THE LORDS OF DEATH

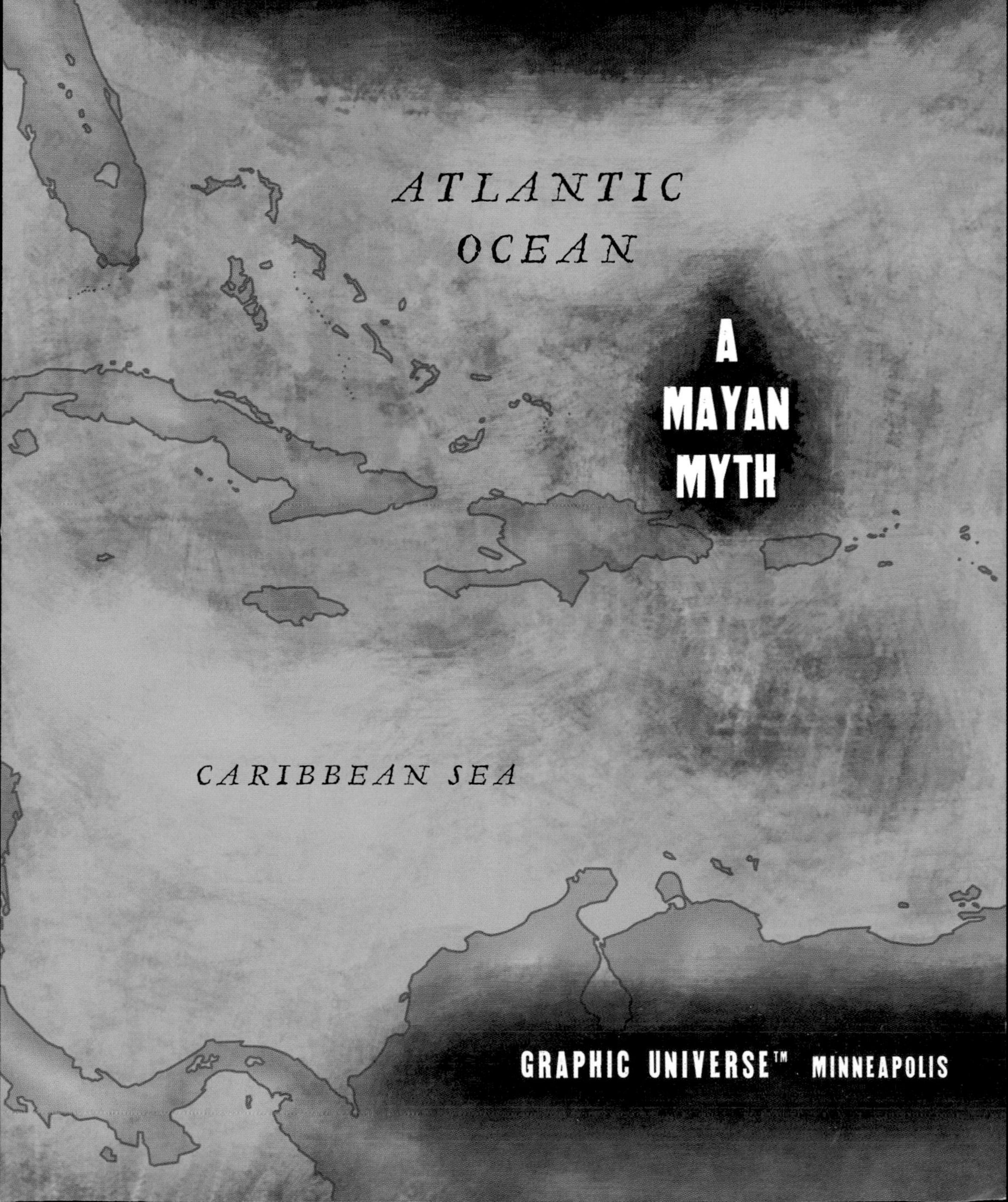
ATLANTIC
OCEAN
CARIBBEAN SEA

A MAYAN MYTH

GRAPHIC UNIVERSE™ MINNEAPOLIS

THE STORY OF THE HERO TWINS, HUNAHPU AND XBALANQUE, IS ONE OF MANY EXCITING TALES FOUND IN THE COLLECTION OF MAYAN STORIES KNOWN AS THE *POPOL VUH*. AUTHOR DAN JOLLEY CONSULTED SEVERAL TRANSLATIONS OF THE *POPOL VUH* TO CREATE THIS EXCITING AND FUNNY BOOK. TO CREATE AUTHENTIC COSTUMING AND SETTING, ARTIST DAVID WITT REVIEWED NUMEROUS BOOKS EXPLORING MAYAN HISTORY, ART, AND ARCHITECTURE. FINALLY, MESOAMERICAN FOLKLORE EXPERT JOHN BIERHORST REVIEWED THE STORY AND THE ARTWORK TO ENSURE ITS AUTHENTICITY AND RESPECT FOR THE MAYAN TRADITION.

STORY BY DAN JOLLEY

PENCILS AND INKS BY DAVID WITT

COLORING BY HI-FI COLOUR DESIGN

LETTERING BY MARSHALL DILLON AND TERRI DELGADO

CONSULTANT: JOHN BIERHORST

Graphic Universe™
A division of Lerner Publishing Group, Inc.
241 First Avenue North
Minneapolis, MN 55401 USA

For reading levels and more information, look up this title at www.lernerbooks.com.

Library of Congress Cataloging-in-Publication Data

Jolley, Dan.
    The hero twins : against the lords of death : a Mayan myth / story by Dan Jolley ; pencils and inks by David Witt.

TABLE OF CONTENTS

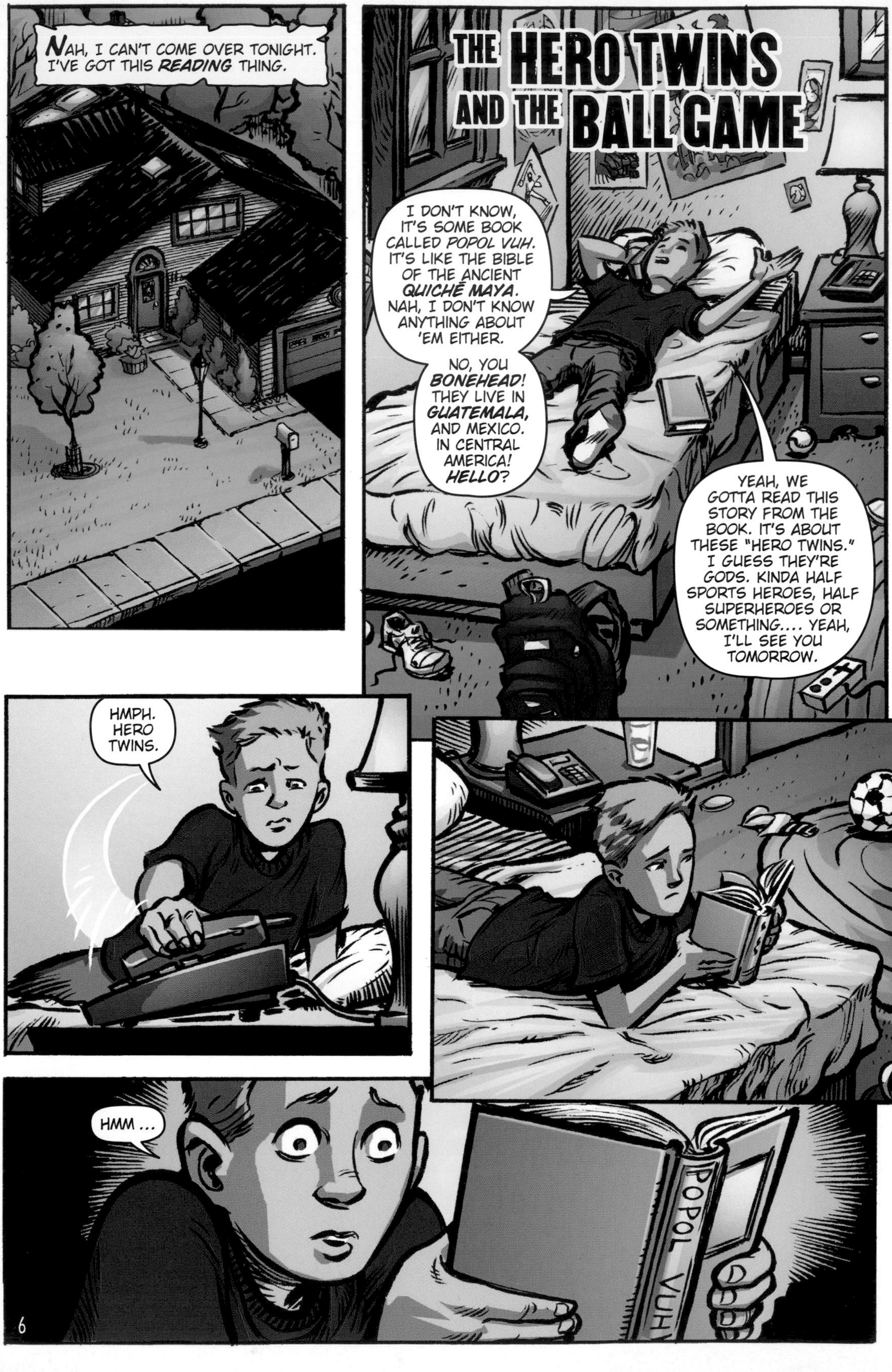

NAH, I CAN'T COME OVER TONIGHT. I'VE GOT THIS READING THING.
THE HERO TWINS AND THE BALL GAME
I DON'T KNOW, IT'S SOME BOOK CALLED POPOL VUH. IT'S LIKE THE BIBLE OF THE ANCIENT QUICHÉ MAYA. NAH, I DON'T KNOW ANYTHING ABOUT 'EM EITHER.
NO, YOU BONEHEAD! THEY LIVE IN GUATEMALA, AND MEXICO. IN CENTRAL AMERICA! HELLO?
YEAH, WE GOTTA READ THIS STORY FROM THE BOOK. IT'S ABOUT THESE "HERO TWINS." I GUESS THEY'RE GODS. KINDA HALF SPORTS HEROES, HALF SUPERHEROES OR SOMETHING.... YEAH, I'LL SEE YOU TOMORROW.
HMPH. HERO TWINS.
HMM ...
POPOL VUH

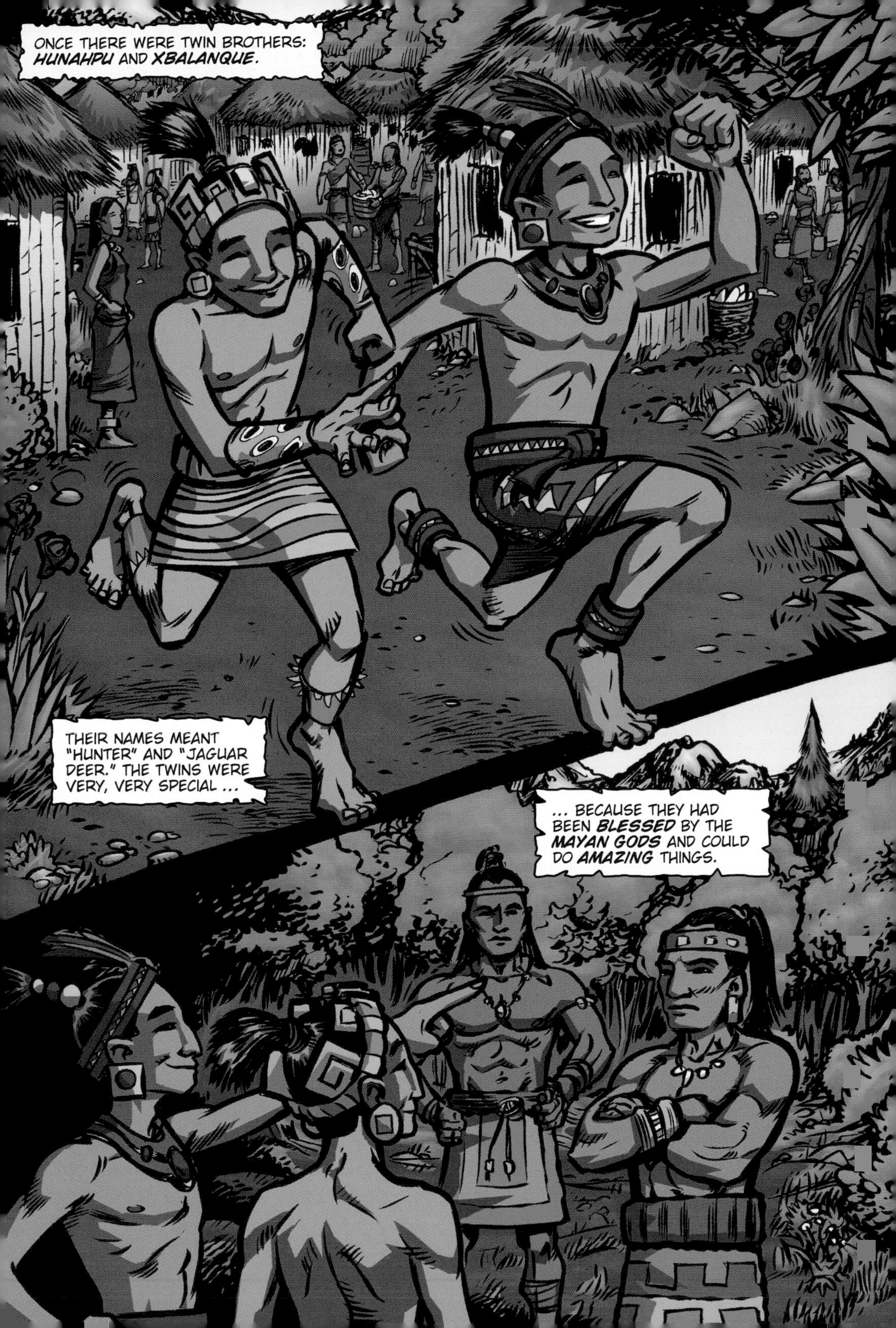
ONCE THERE WERE TWIN BROTHERS: HUNAHPU AND XBALANQUE.
THEIR NAMES MEANT "HUNTER" AND "JAGUAR DEER." THE TWINS WERE VERY, VERY SPECIAL ...
... BECAUSE THEY HAD BEEN BLESSED BY THE MAYAN GODS AND COULD DO AMAZING THINGS.

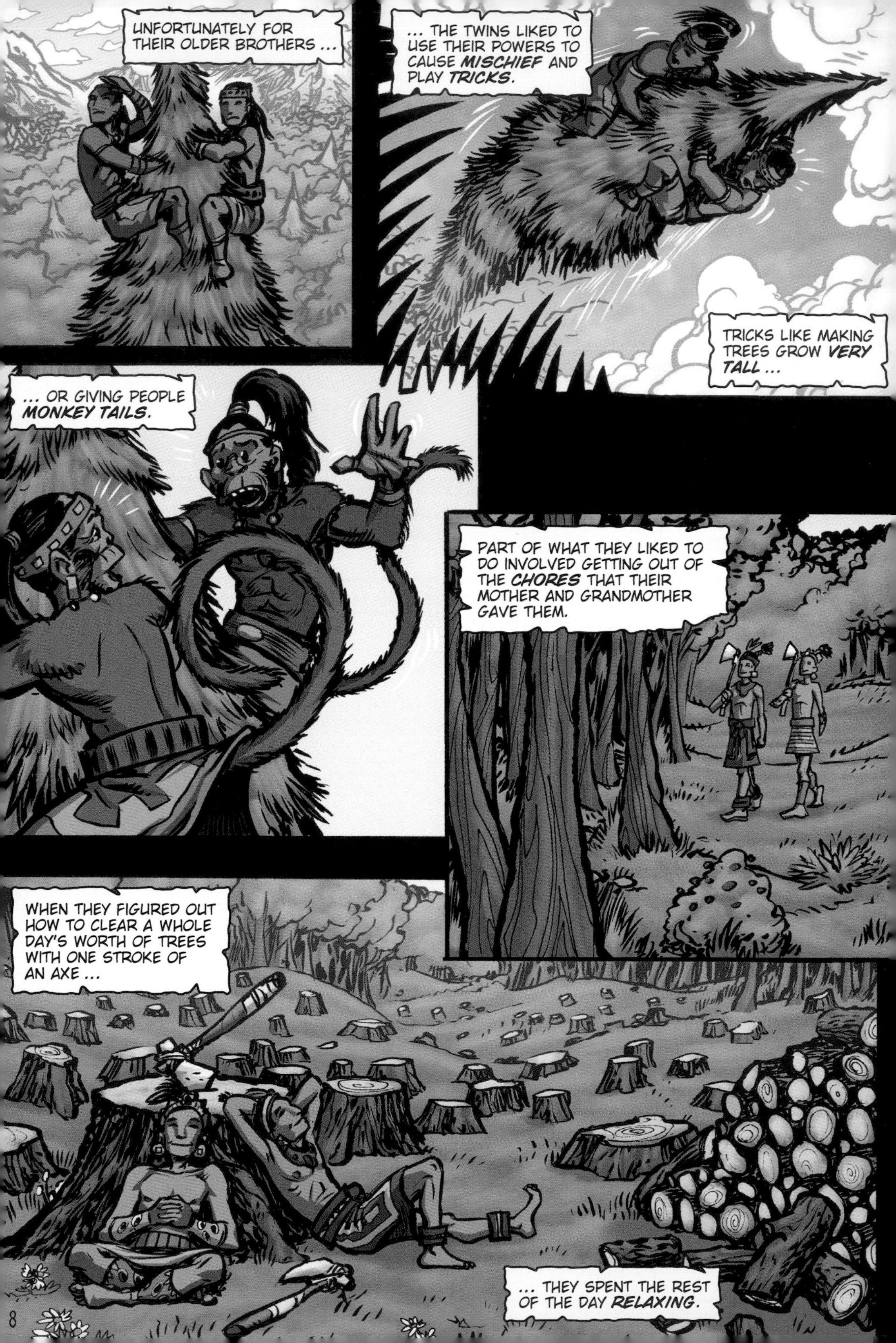
UNFORTUNATELY FOR THEIR OLDER BROTHERS ...
... THE TWINS LIKED TO USE THEIR POWERS TO CAUSE **MISCHIEF** AND PLAY **TRICKS**.
TRICKS LIKE MAKING TREES GROW **VERY TALL** ...
... OR GIVING PEOPLE **MONKEY TAILS**.
PART OF WHAT THEY LIKED TO DO INVOLVED GETTING OUT OF THE **CHORES** THAT THEIR MOTHER AND GRANDMOTHER GAVE THEM.
WHEN THEY FIGURED OUT HOW TO CLEAR A WHOLE DAY'S WORTH OF TREES WITH ONE STROKE OF AN AXE ...
... THEY SPENT THE REST OF THE DAY **RELAXING**.

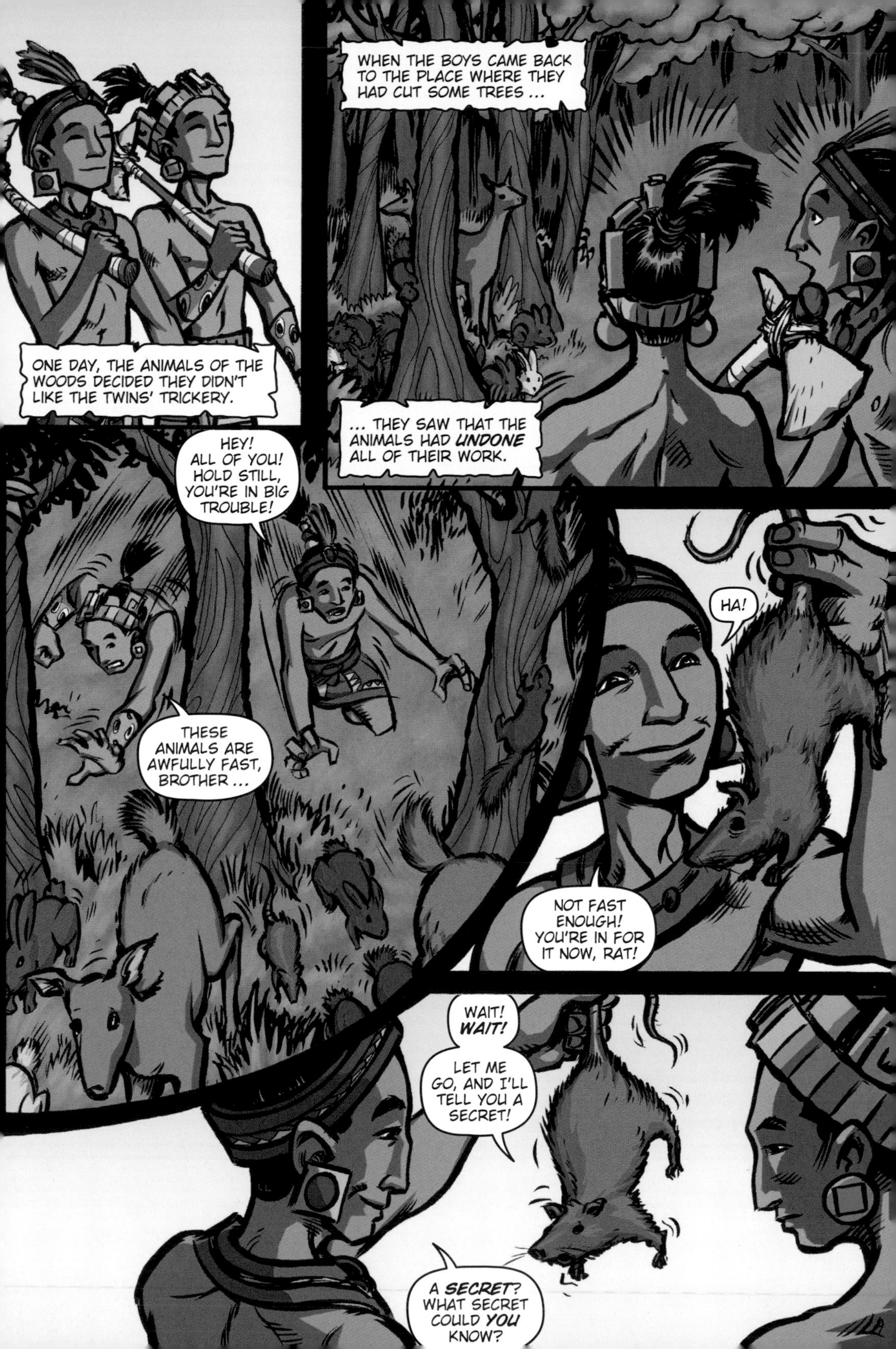

ONE DAY, THE ANIMALS OF THE WOODS DECIDED THEY DIDN'T LIKE THE TWINS' TRICKERY.
WHEN THE BOYS CAME BACK TO THE PLACE WHERE THEY HAD CUT SOME TREES ...
... THEY SAW THAT THE ANIMALS HAD UNDONE ALL OF THEIR WORK.
HEY! ALL OF YOU! HOLD STILL, YOU'RE IN BIG TROUBLE!
THESE ANIMALS ARE AWFULLY FAST, BROTHER ...
HA!
NOT FAST ENOUGH! YOU'RE IN FOR IT NOW, RAT!
WAIT! WAIT!
LET ME GO, AND I'LL TELL YOU A SECRET!
A SECRET? WHAT SECRET COULD YOU KNOW?

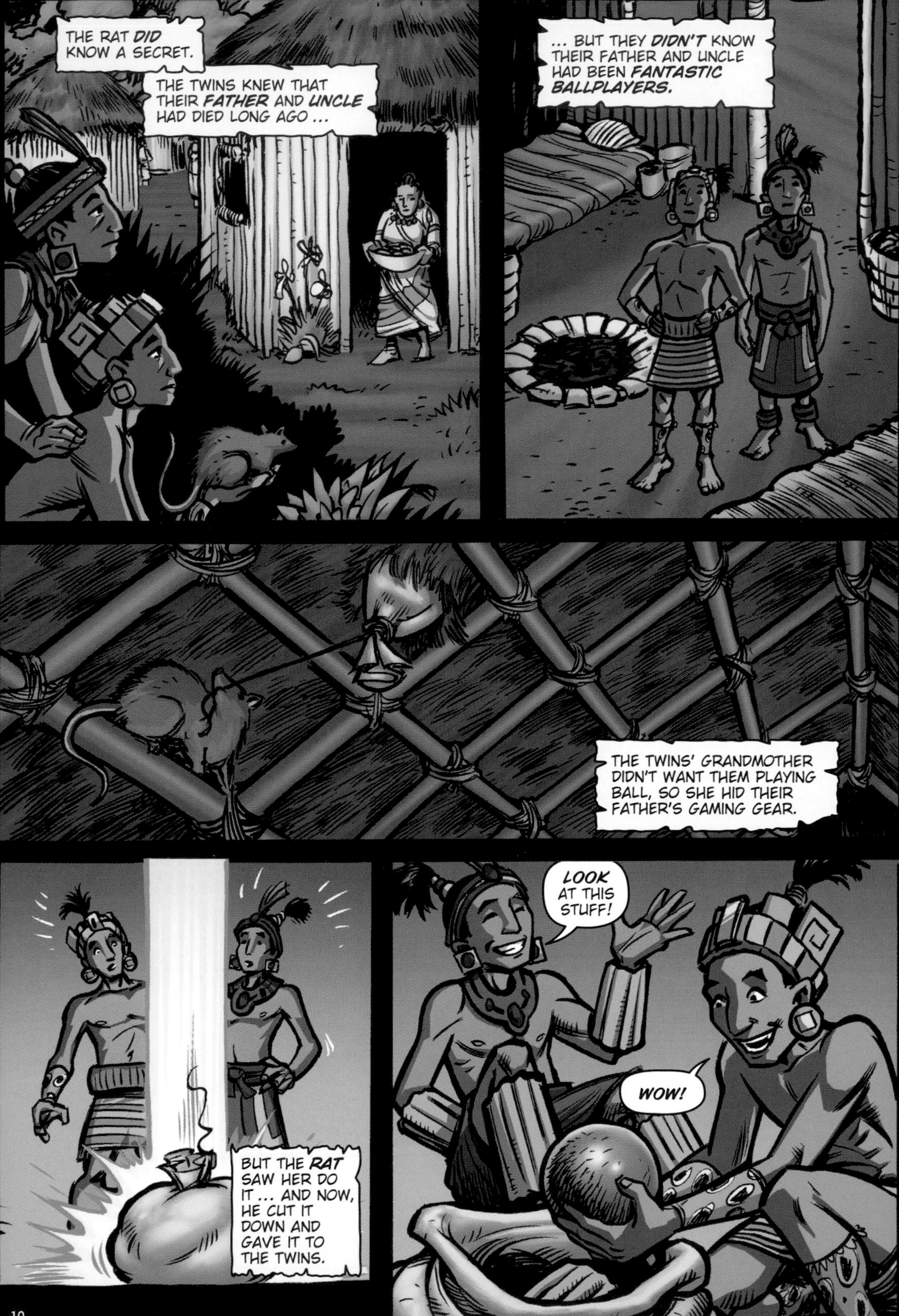
THE RAT DID KNOW A SECRET.
THE TWINS KNEW THAT THEIR FATHER AND UNCLE HAD DIED LONG AGO ...
... BUT THEY DIDN'T KNOW THEIR FATHER AND UNCLE HAD BEEN FANTASTIC BALLPLAYERS.
THE TWINS' GRANDMOTHER DIDN'T WANT THEM PLAYING BALL, SO SHE HID THEIR FATHER'S GAMING GEAR.
BUT THE RAT SAW HER DO IT ... AND NOW, HE CUT IT DOWN AND GAVE IT TO THE TWINS.
LOOK AT THIS STUFF!
WOW!

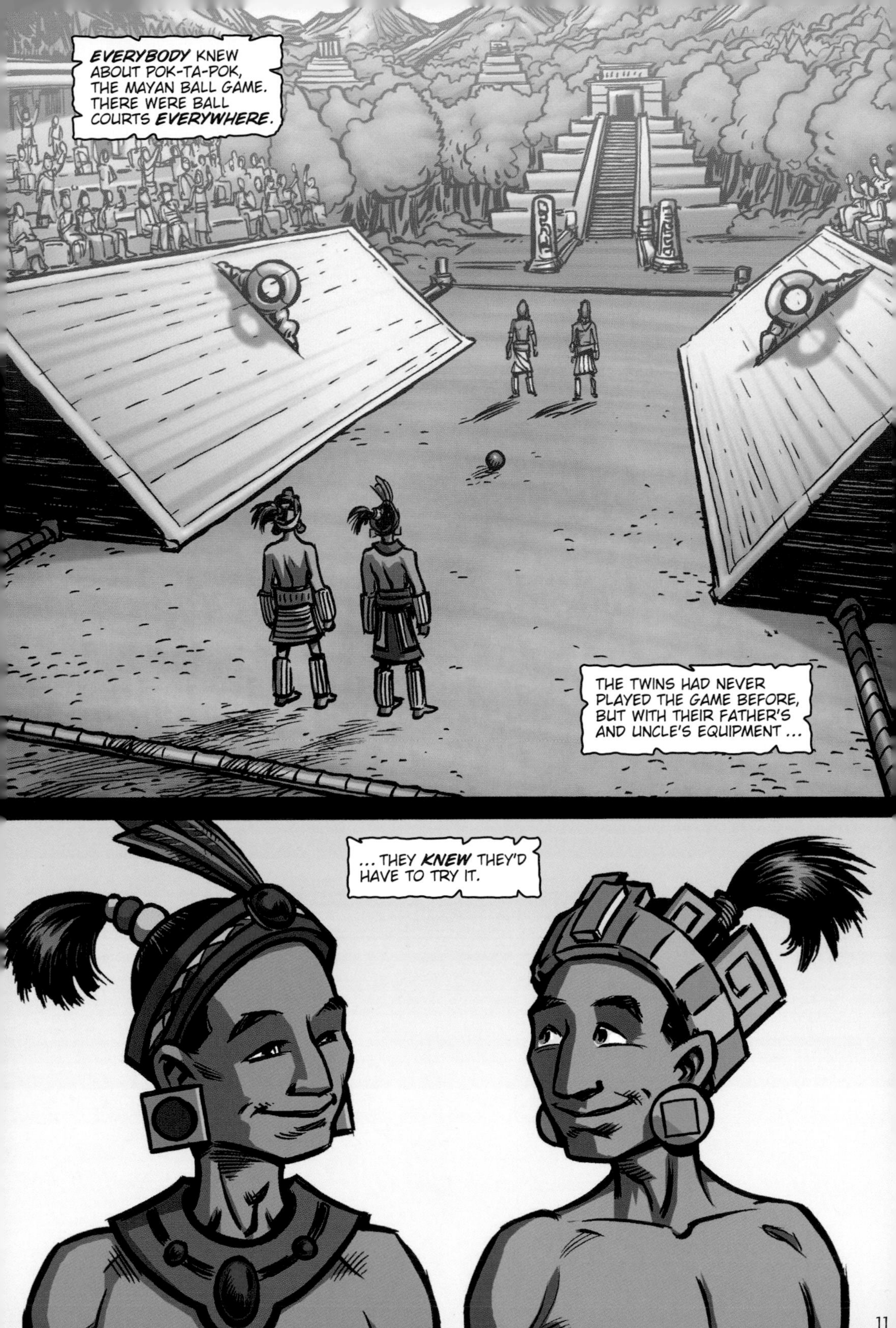
EVERYBODY KNEW ABOUT POK-TA-POK, THE MAYAN BALL GAME. THERE WERE BALL COURTS EVERYWHERE.
THE TWINS HAD NEVER PLAYED THE GAME BEFORE, BUT WITH THEIR FATHER'S AND UNCLE'S EQUIPMENT ...
... THEY KNEW THEY'D HAVE TO TRY IT.

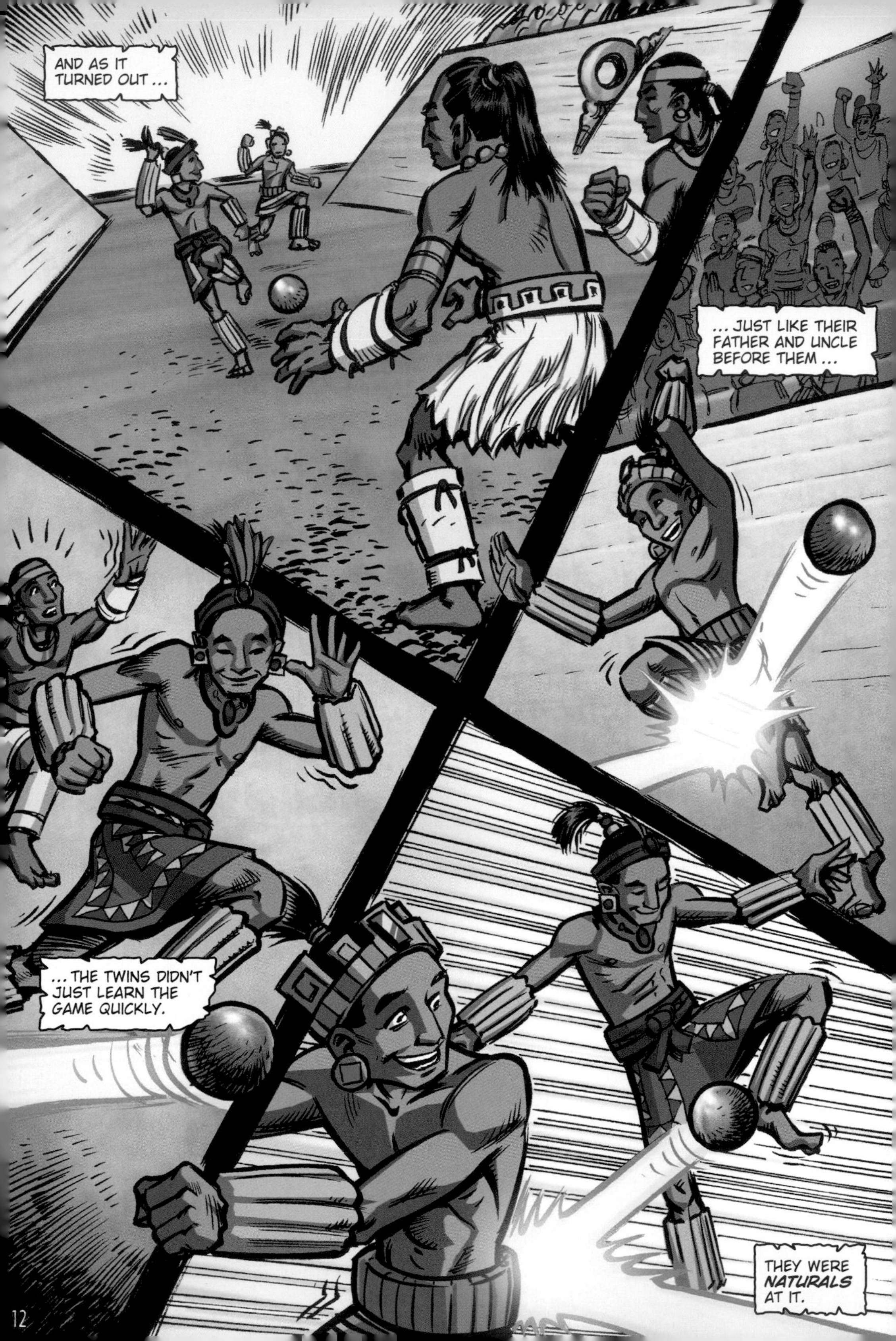
AND AS IT TURNED OUT . . .
. . . JUST LIKE THEIR FATHER AND UNCLE BEFORE THEM . . .
. . . THE TWINS DIDN'T JUST LEARN THE GAME QUICKLY.
THEY WERE *NATURALS* AT IT.

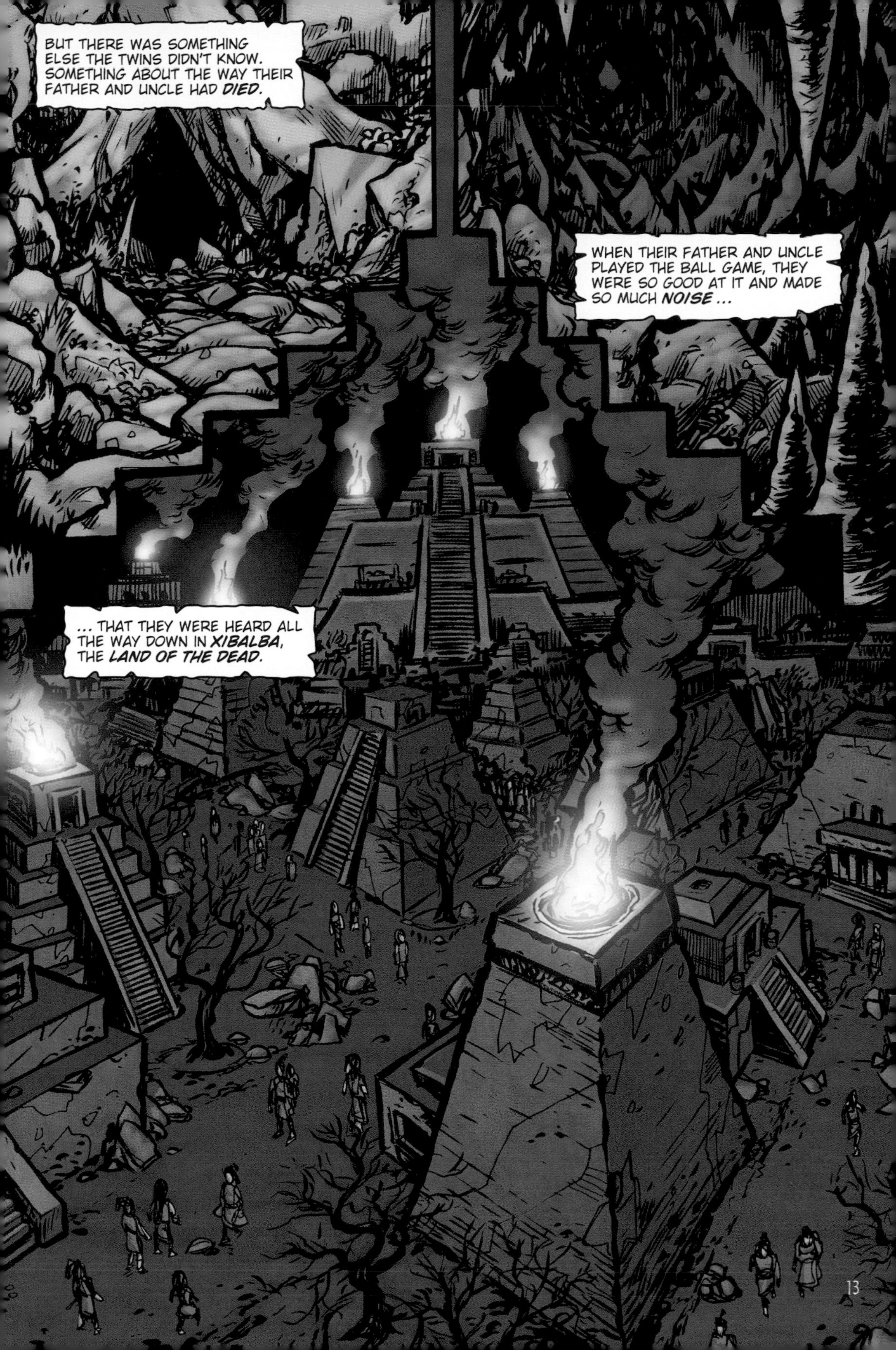
BUT THERE WAS SOMETHING ELSE THE TWINS DIDN'T KNOW. SOMETHING ABOUT THE WAY THEIR FATHER AND UNCLE HAD ***DIED***.
WHEN THEIR FATHER AND UNCLE PLAYED THE BALL GAME, THEY WERE SO GOOD AT IT AND MADE SO MUCH ***NOISE*** ...
... THAT THEY WERE HEARD ALL THE WAY DOWN IN ***XIBALBA***, THE ***LAND OF THE DEAD***.

THE LORDS OF XIBALBA

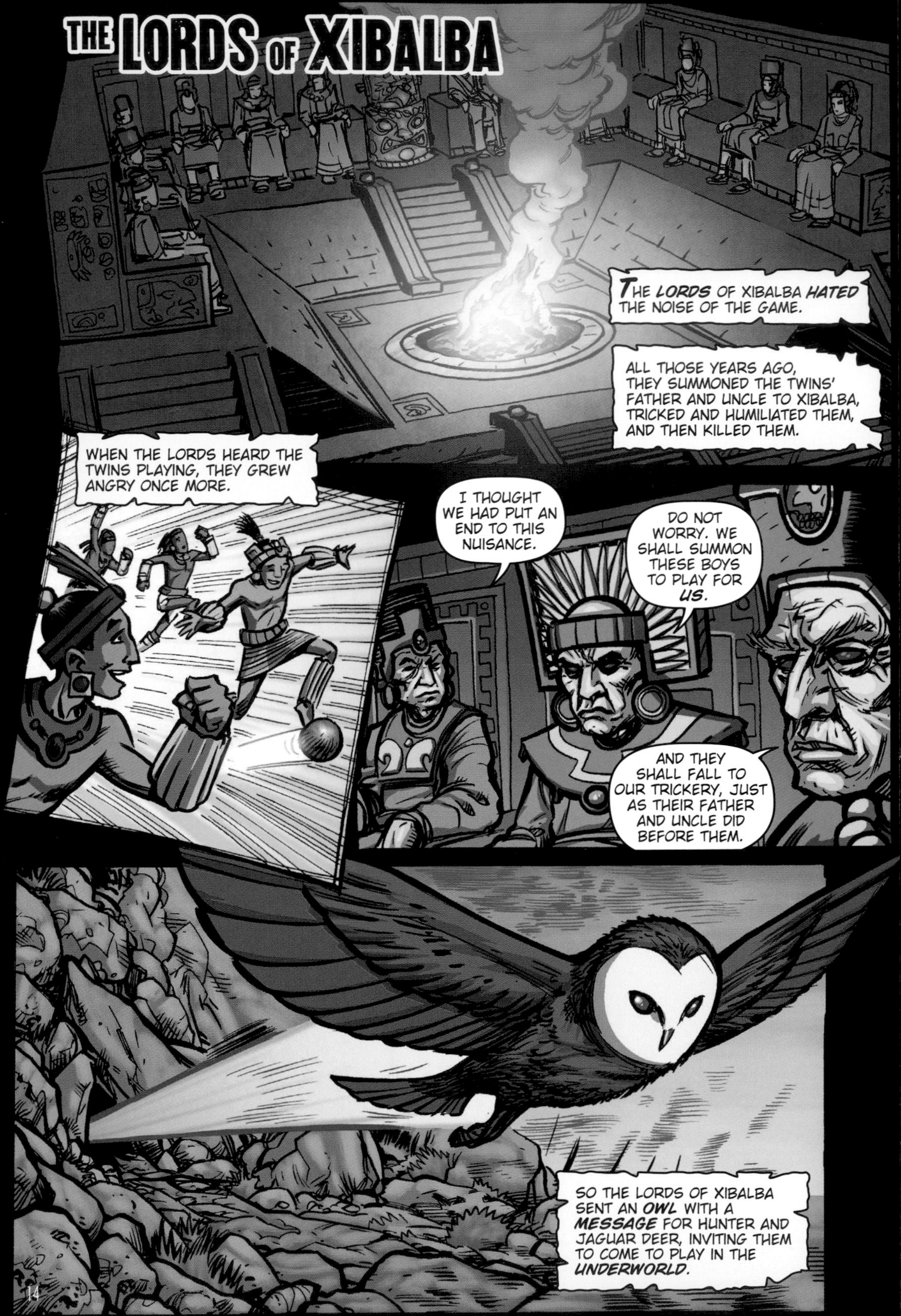
THE LORDS OF XIBALBA HATED THE NOISE OF THE GAME.
ALL THOSE YEARS AGO, THEY SUMMONED THE TWINS' FATHER AND UNCLE TO XIBALBA, TRICKED AND HUMILIATED THEM, AND THEN KILLED THEM.
WHEN THE LORDS HEARD THE TWINS PLAYING, THEY GREW ANGRY ONCE MORE.
I THOUGHT WE HAD PUT AN END TO THIS NUISANCE.
DO NOT WORRY. WE SHALL SUMMON THESE BOYS TO PLAY FOR US.
AND THEY SHALL FALL TO OUR TRICKERY, JUST AS THEIR FATHER AND UNCLE DID BEFORE THEM.
SO THE LORDS OF XIBALBA SENT AN OWL WITH A MESSAGE FOR HUNTER AND JAGUAR DEER, INVITING THEM TO COME TO PLAY IN THE UNDERWORLD.

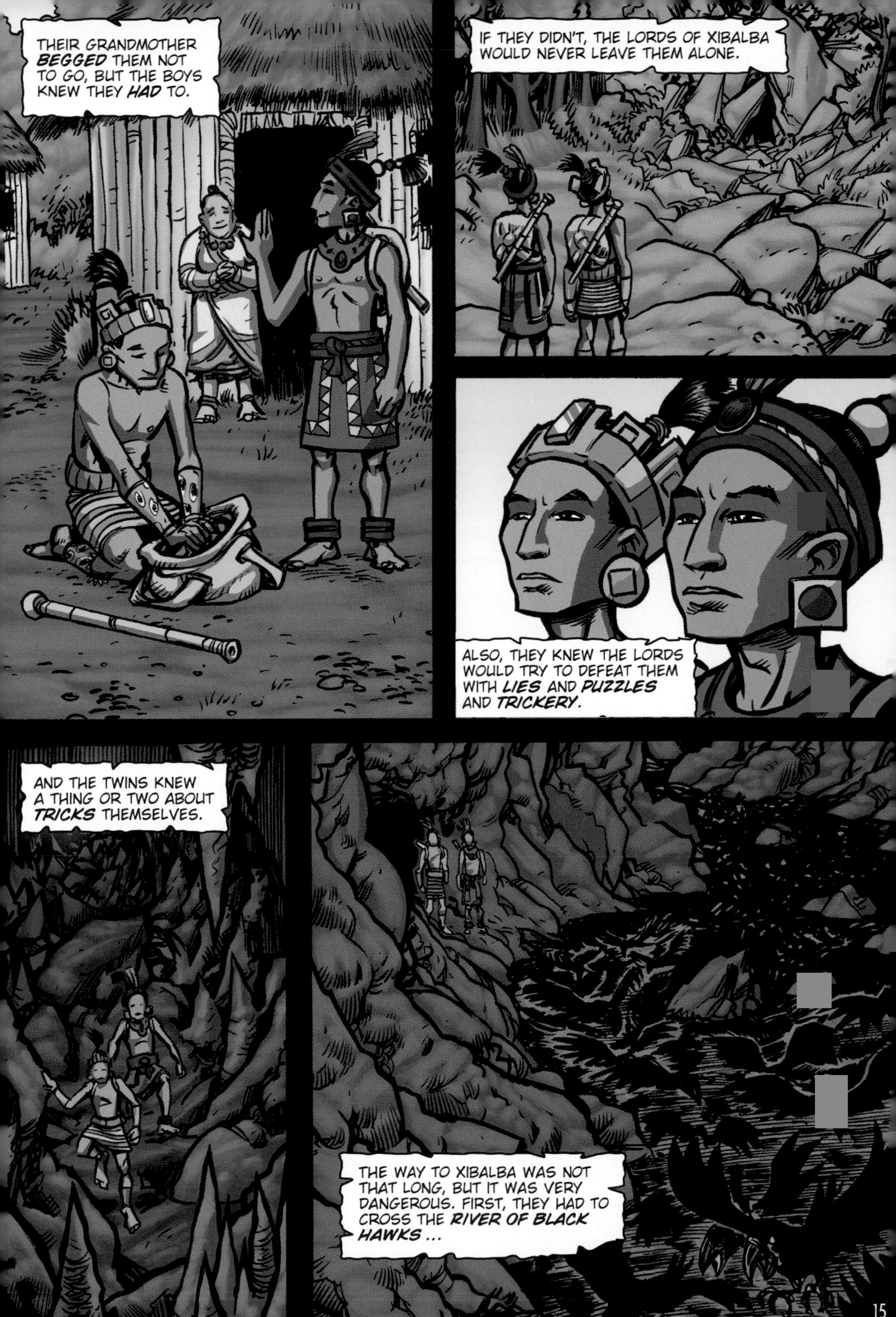
THEIR GRANDMOTHER BEGGED THEM NOT TO GO, BUT THE BOYS KNEW THEY HAD TO.
IF THEY DIDN'T, THE LORDS OF XIBALBA WOULD NEVER LEAVE THEM ALONE.
ALSO, THEY KNEW THE LORDS WOULD TRY TO DEFEAT THEM WITH LIES AND PUZZLES AND TRICKERY.
AND THE TWINS KNEW A THING OR TWO ABOUT TRICKS THEMSELVES.
THE WAY TO XIBALBA WAS NOT THAT LONG, BUT IT WAS VERY DANGEROUS. FIRST, THEY HAD TO CROSS THE RIVER OF BLACK HAWKS . . .

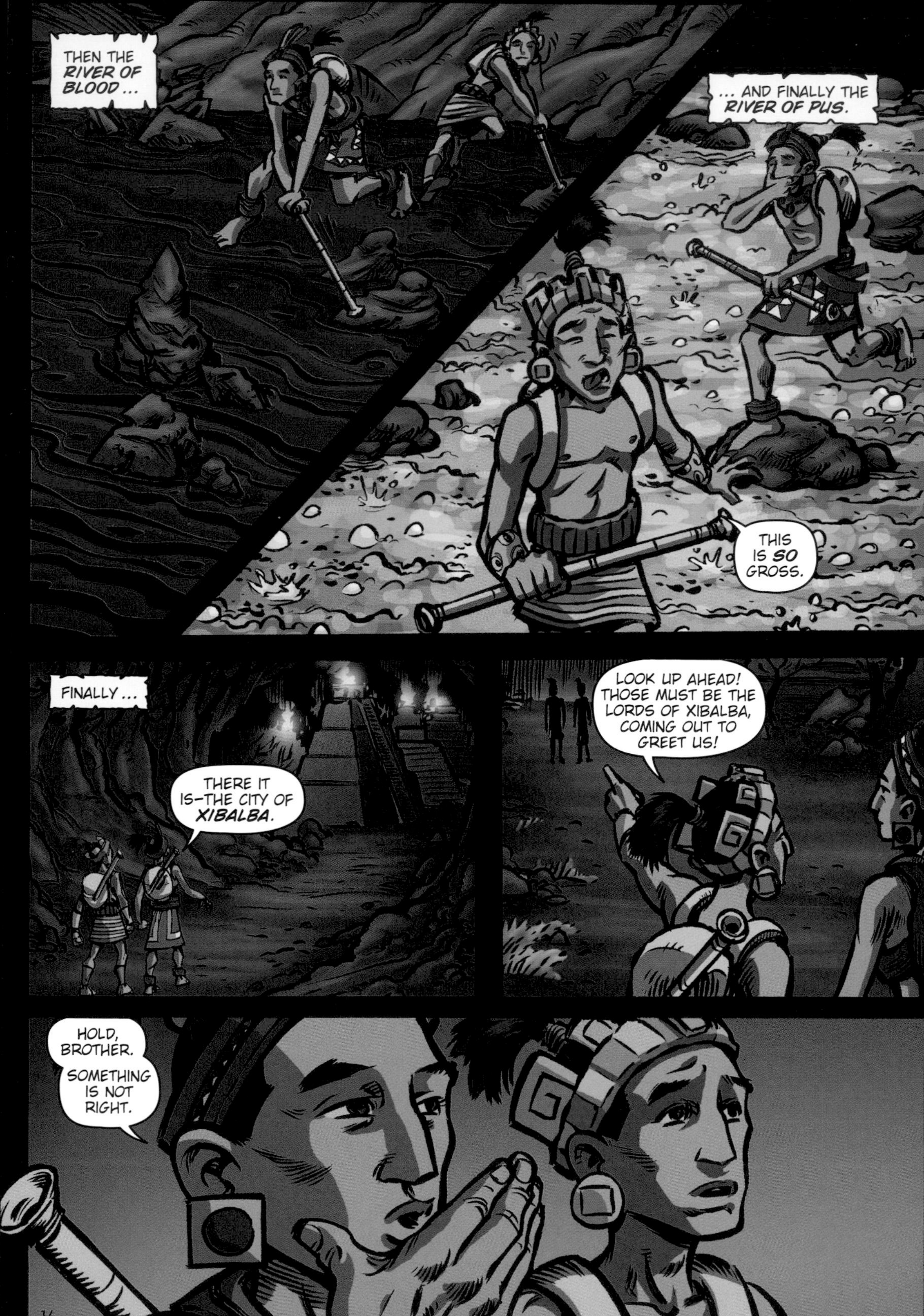

THEN THE *RIVER OF BLOOD* ...
... AND FINALLY THE *RIVER OF PUS*.
THIS IS **SO** GROSS.
FINALLY ...
THERE IT IS—THE CITY OF ***XIBALBA***.
LOOK UP AHEAD! THOSE MUST BE THE LORDS OF XIBALBA, COMING OUT TO GREET US!
HOLD, BROTHER.
SOMETHING IS NOT RIGHT.

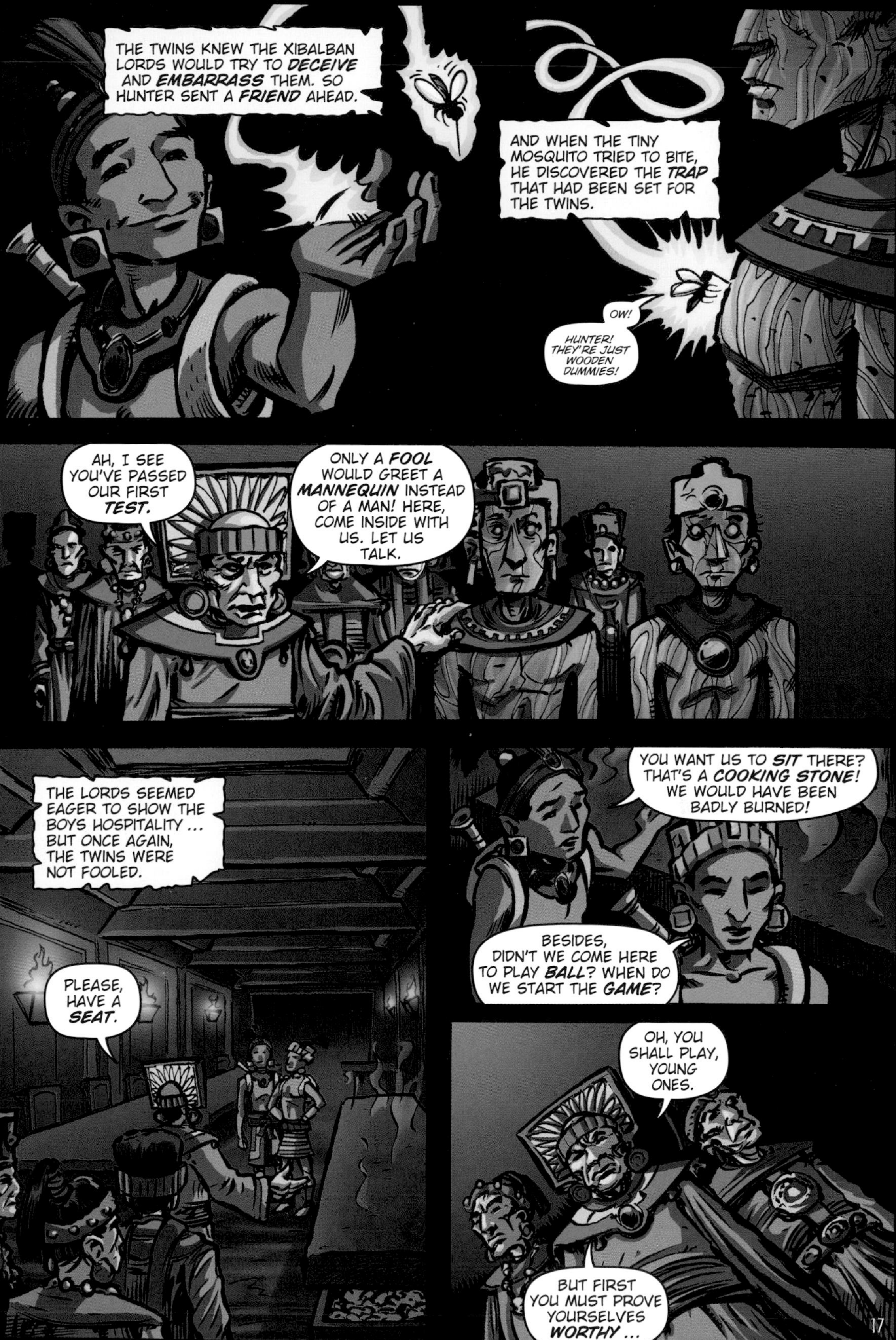
THE TWINS KNEW THE XIBALBAN LORDS WOULD TRY TO DECEIVE AND EMBARRASS THEM. SO HUNTER SENT A FRIEND AHEAD.
AND WHEN THE TINY MOSQUITO TRIED TO BITE, HE DISCOVERED THE TRAP THAT HAD BEEN SET FOR THE TWINS.
OW!
HUNTER! THEY'RE JUST WOODEN DUMMIES!
AH, I SEE YOU'VE PASSED OUR FIRST TEST.
ONLY A FOOL WOULD GREET A MANNEQUIN INSTEAD OF A MAN! HERE, COME INSIDE WITH US. LET US TALK.
THE LORDS SEEMED EAGER TO SHOW THE BOYS HOSPITALITY ... BUT ONCE AGAIN, THE TWINS WERE NOT FOOLED.
PLEASE, HAVE A SEAT.
YOU WANT US TO SIT THERE? THAT'S A COOKING STONE! WE WOULD HAVE BEEN BADLY BURNED!
BESIDES, DIDN'T WE COME HERE TO PLAY BALL? WHEN DO WE START THE GAME?
OH, YOU SHALL PLAY, YOUNG ONES.
BUT FIRST YOU MUST PROVE YOURSELVES WORTHY ...

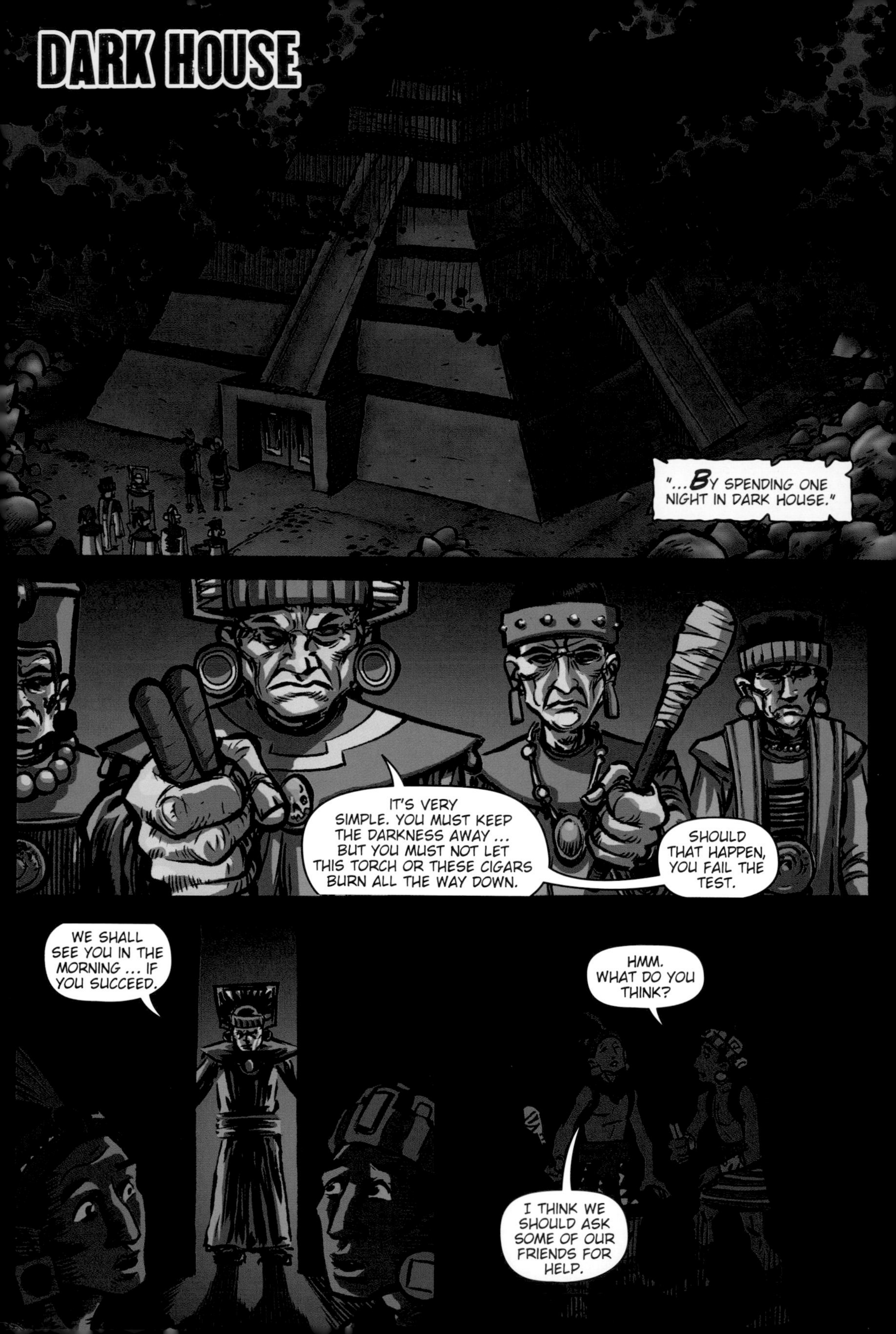
DARK HOUSE
"...BY SPENDING ONE NIGHT IN DARK HOUSE."
IT'S VERY SIMPLE. YOU MUST KEEP THE DARKNESS AWAY ... BUT YOU MUST NOT LET THIS TORCH OR THESE CIGARS BURN ALL THE WAY DOWN.
SHOULD THAT HAPPEN, YOU FAIL THE TEST.
WE SHALL SEE YOU IN THE MORNING ... IF YOU SUCCEED.
HMM. WHAT DO YOU THINK?
I THINK WE SHOULD ASK SOME OF OUR FRIENDS FOR HELP.

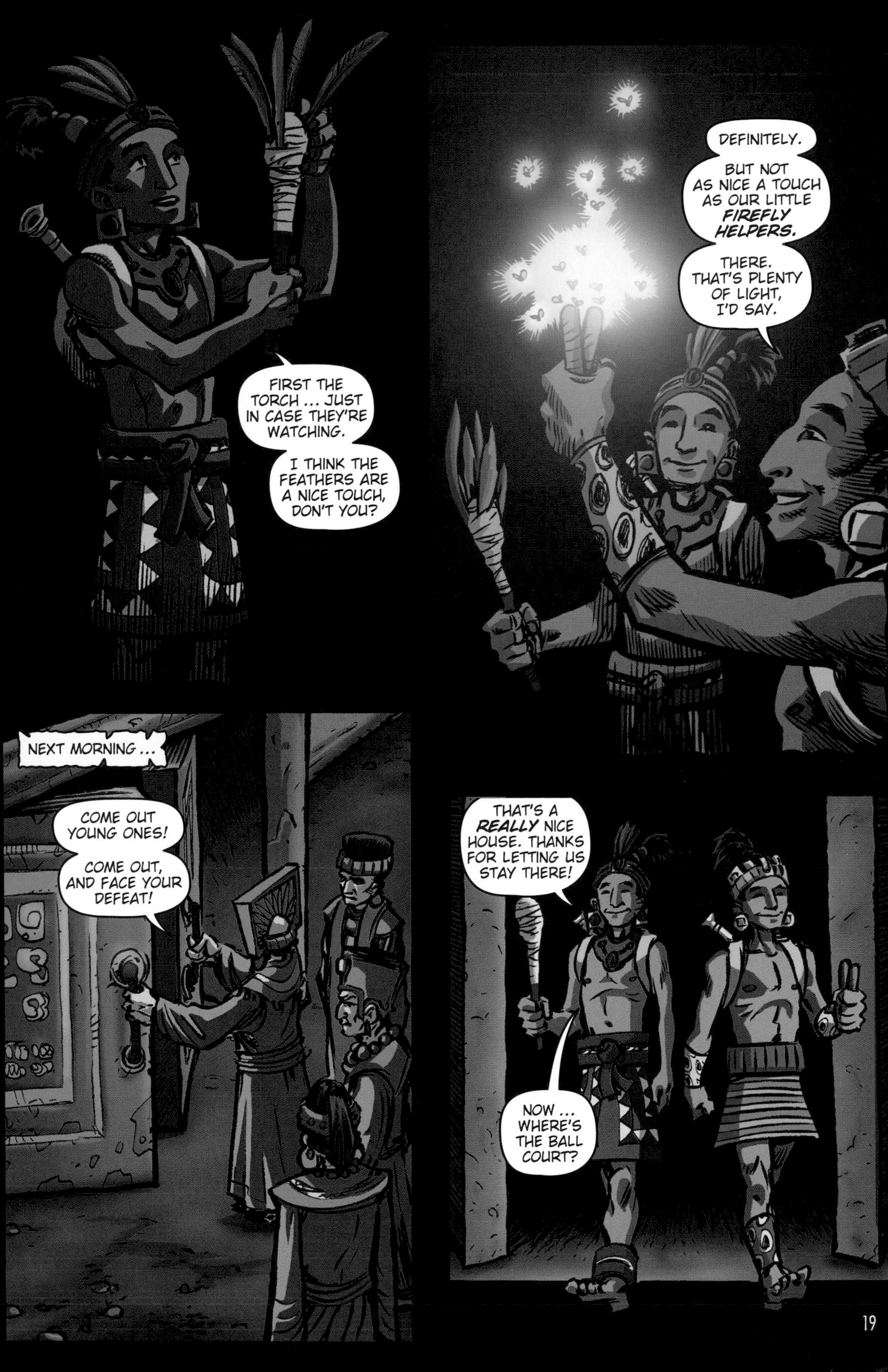
FIRST THE TORCH ... JUST IN CASE THEY'RE WATCHING.
I THINK THE FEATHERS ARE A NICE TOUCH, DON'T YOU?
DEFINITELY.
BUT NOT AS NICE A TOUCH AS OUR LITTLE FIREFLY HELPERS.
THERE. THAT'S PLENTY OF LIGHT, I'D SAY.
NEXT MORNING ...
COME OUT YOUNG ONES!
COME OUT, AND FACE YOUR DEFEAT!
THAT'S A REALLY NICE HOUSE. THANKS FOR LETTING US STAY THERE!
NOW ... WHERE'S THE BALL COURT?

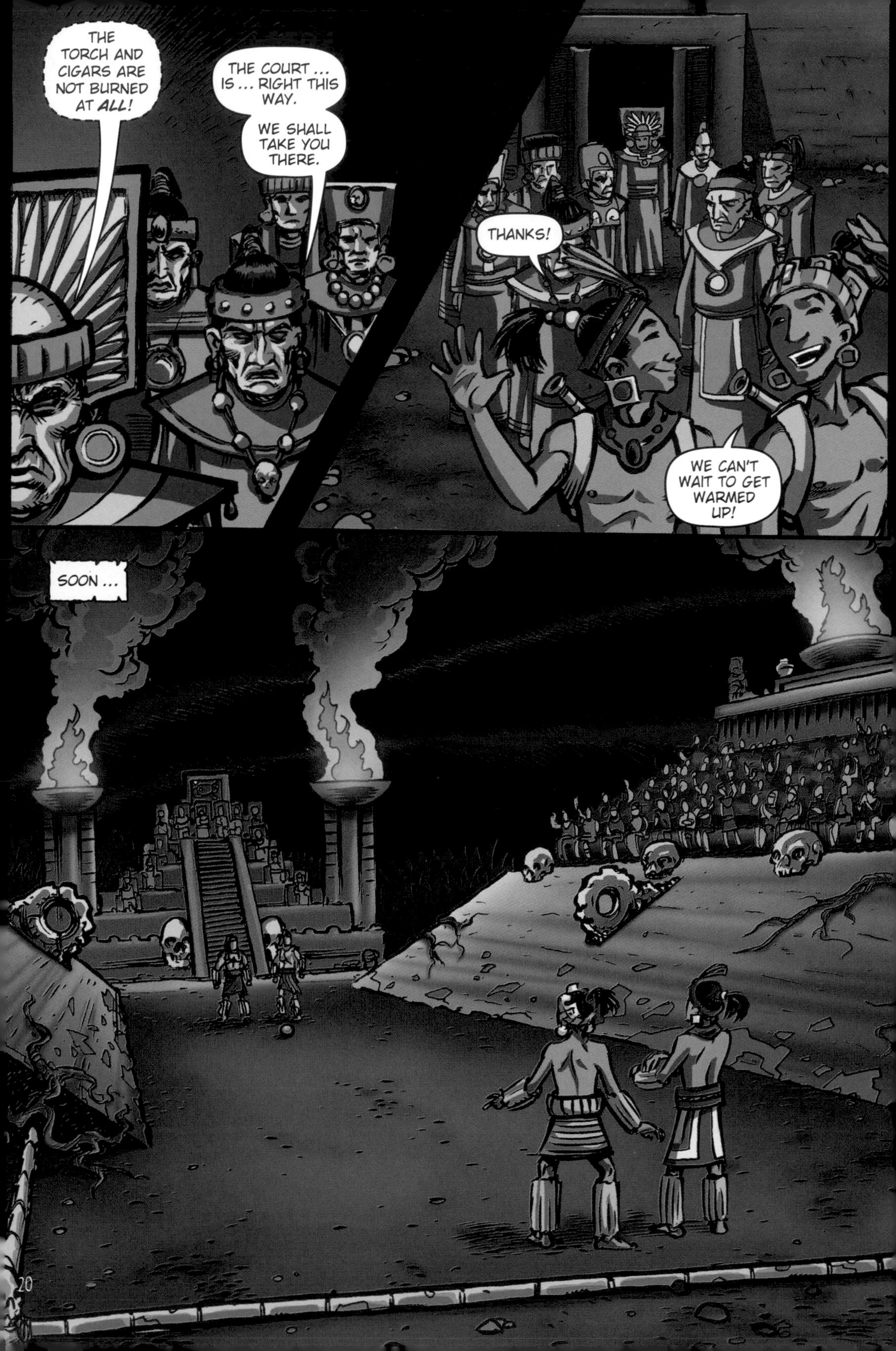
THE TORCH AND CIGARS ARE NOT BURNED AT ALL!
THE COURT ... IS ... RIGHT THIS WAY.
WE SHALL TAKE YOU THERE.
THANKS!
WE CAN'T WAIT TO GET WARMED UP!
SOON ...

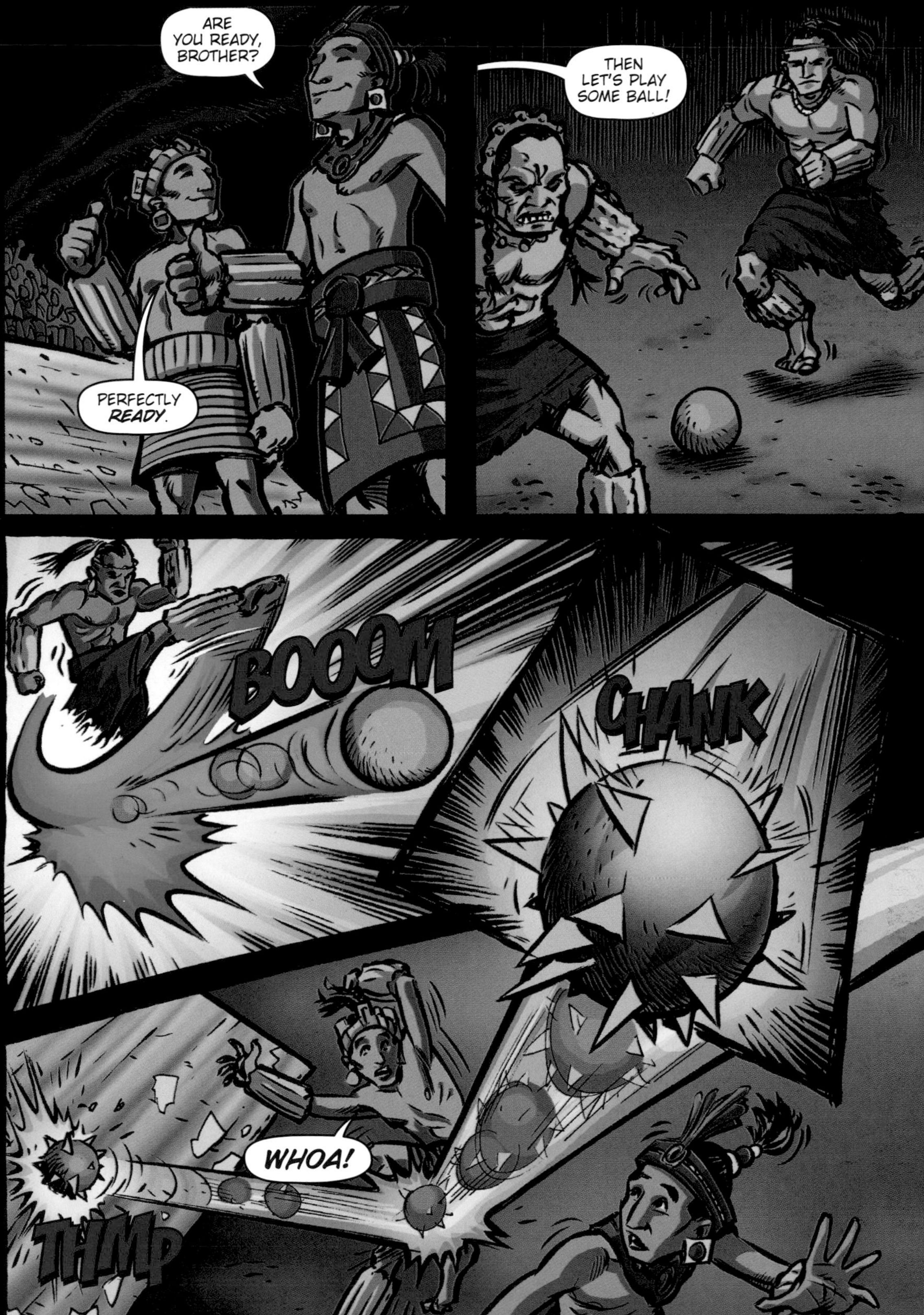
ARE YOU READY, BROTHER?
PERFECTLY *READY*.
THEN LET'S PLAY SOME BALL!
BOOOM
CHANK
WHOA!
THIMP

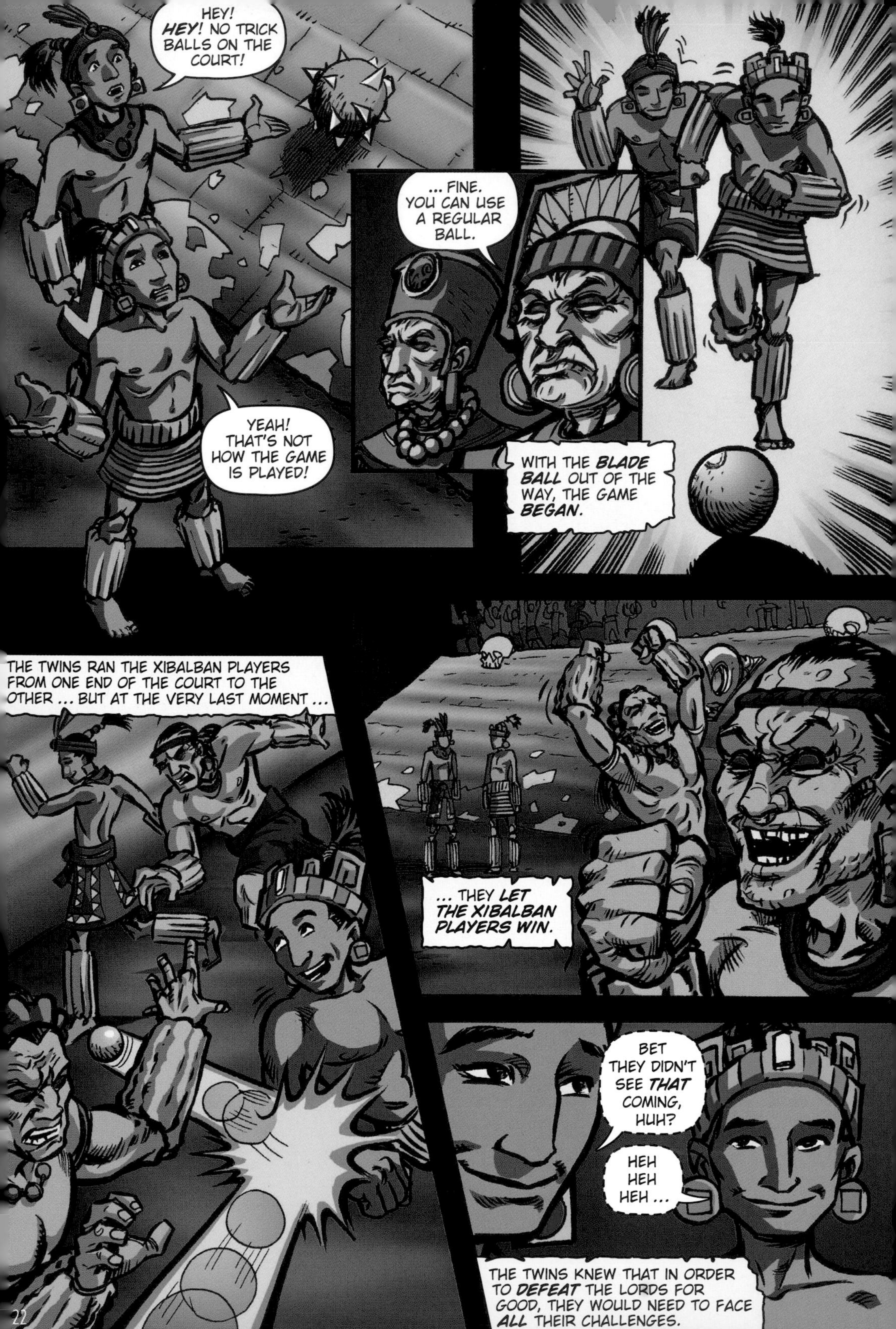
HEY! HEY! NO TRICK BALLS ON THE COURT!
YEAH! THAT'S NOT HOW THE GAME IS PLAYED!
... FINE. YOU CAN USE A REGULAR BALL.
WITH THE BLADE BALL OUT OF THE WAY, THE GAME BEGAN.
THE TWINS RAN THE XIBALBAN PLAYERS FROM ONE END OF THE COURT TO THE OTHER ... BUT AT THE VERY LAST MOMENT ...
... THEY LET THE XIBALBAN PLAYERS WIN.
BET THEY DIDN'T SEE THAT COMING, HUH?
HEH HEH HEH ...
THE TWINS KNEW THAT IN ORDER TO DEFEAT THE LORDS FOR GOOD, THEY WOULD NEED TO FACE ALL THEIR CHALLENGES.

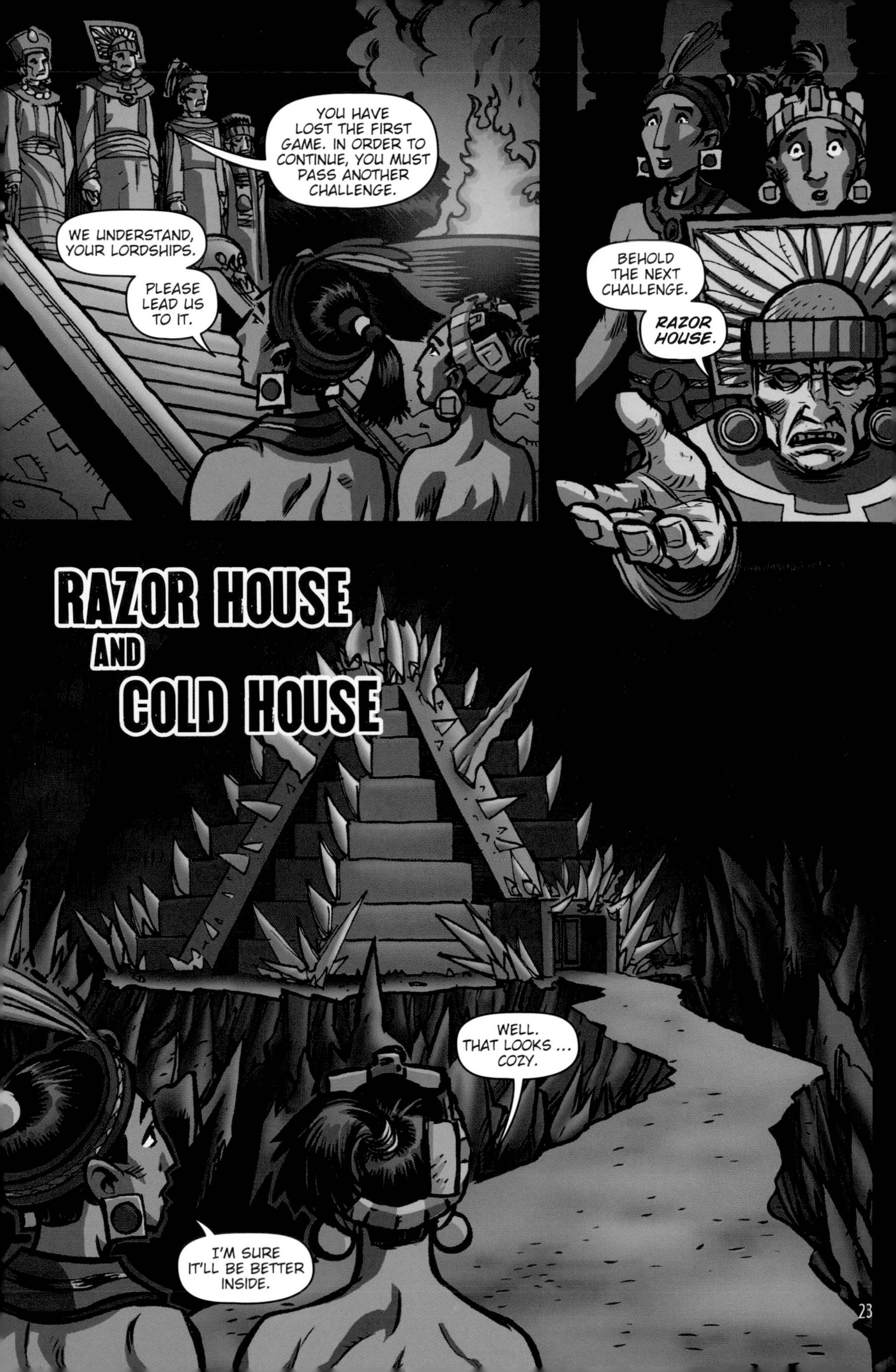
YOU HAVE LOST THE FIRST GAME. IN ORDER TO CONTINUE, YOU MUST PASS ANOTHER CHALLENGE.
WE UNDERSTAND, YOUR LORDSHIPS.
PLEASE LEAD US TO IT.
BEHOLD THE NEXT CHALLENGE.
RAZOR HOUSE.
RAZOR HOUSE AND COLD HOUSE
WELL. THAT LOOKS ... COZY.
I'M SURE IT'LL BE BETTER INSIDE.

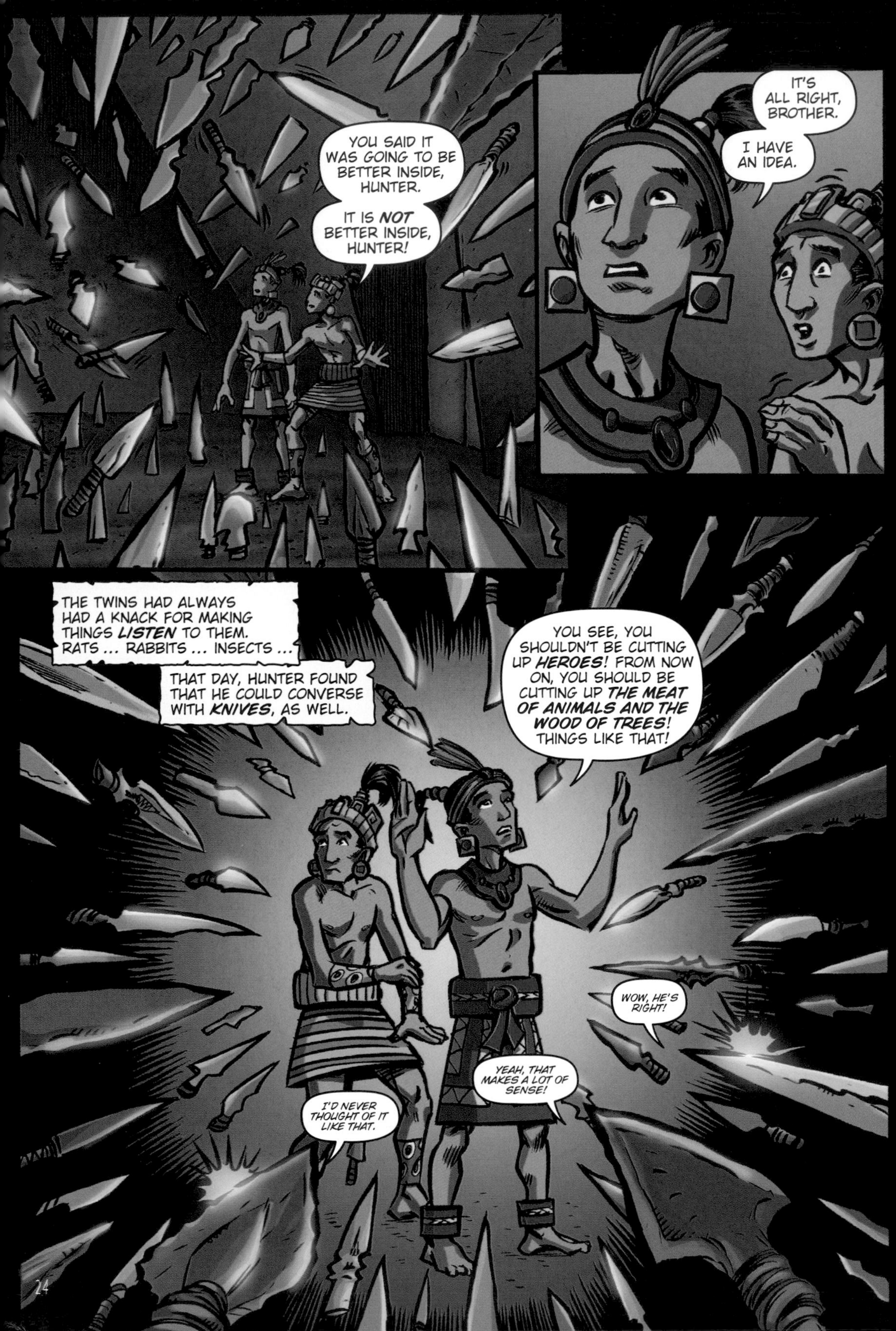
YOU SAID IT WAS GOING TO BE BETTER INSIDE, HUNTER.
IT IS NOT BETTER INSIDE, HUNTER!
IT'S ALL RIGHT, BROTHER.
I HAVE AN IDEA.
THE TWINS HAD ALWAYS HAD A KNACK FOR MAKING THINGS LISTEN TO THEM. RATS ... RABBITS ... INSECTS ...
THAT DAY, HUNTER FOUND THAT HE COULD CONVERSE WITH KNIVES, AS WELL.
YOU SEE, YOU SHOULDN'T BE CUTTING UP HEROES! FROM NOW ON, YOU SHOULD BE CUTTING UP THE MEAT OF ANIMALS AND THE WOOD OF TREES! THINGS LIKE THAT!
WOW, HE'S RIGHT!
YEAH, THAT MAKES A LOT OF SENSE!
I'D NEVER THOUGHT OF IT LIKE THAT.

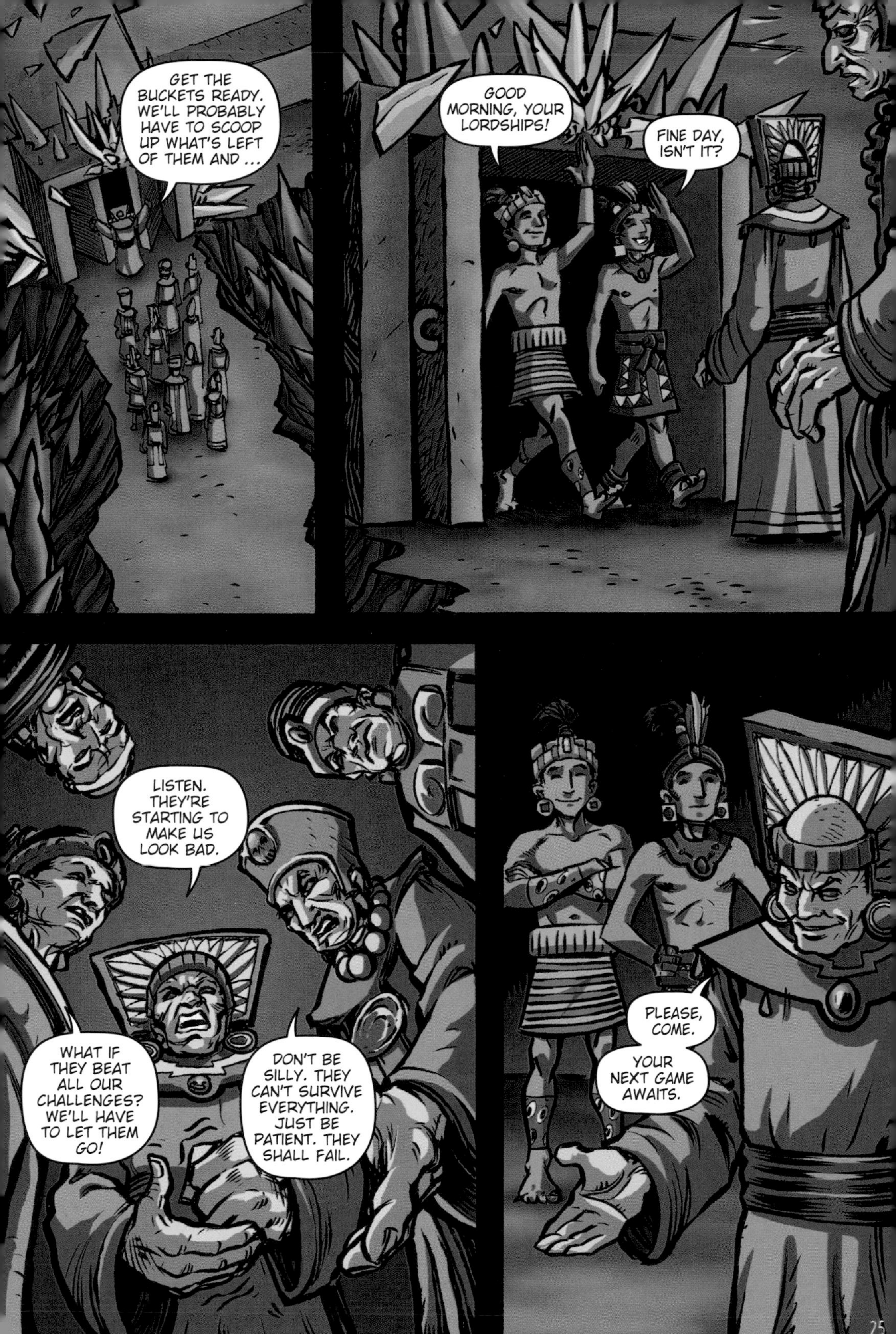
GET THE BUCKETS READY. WE'LL PROBABLY HAVE TO SCOOP UP WHAT'S LEFT OF THEM AND ...
GOOD MORNING, YOUR LORDSHIPS!
FINE DAY, ISN'T IT?
LISTEN. THEY'RE STARTING TO MAKE US LOOK BAD.
WHAT IF THEY BEAT ALL OUR CHALLENGES? WE'LL HAVE TO LET THEM GO!
DON'T BE SILLY. THEY CAN'T SURVIVE EVERYTHING. JUST BE PATIENT. THEY SHALL FAIL.
PLEASE, COME.
YOUR NEXT GAME AWAITS.

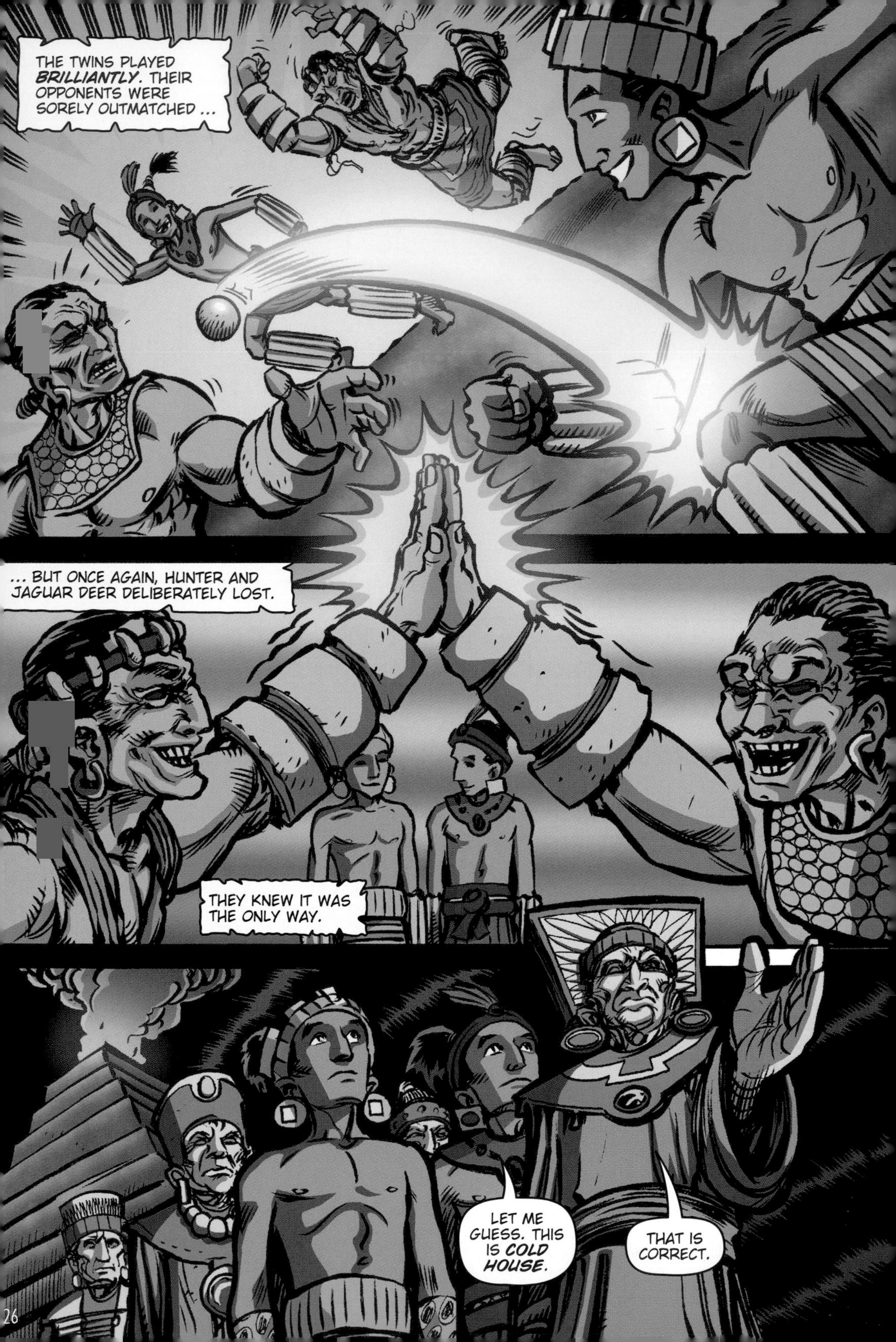
THE TWINS PLAYED BRILLIANTLY. THEIR OPPONENTS WERE SORELY OUTMATCHED ...
... BUT ONCE AGAIN, HUNTER AND JAGUAR DEER DELIBERATELY LOST.
THEY KNEW IT WAS THE ONLY WAY.
LET ME GUESS. THIS IS COLD HOUSE.
THAT IS CORRECT.

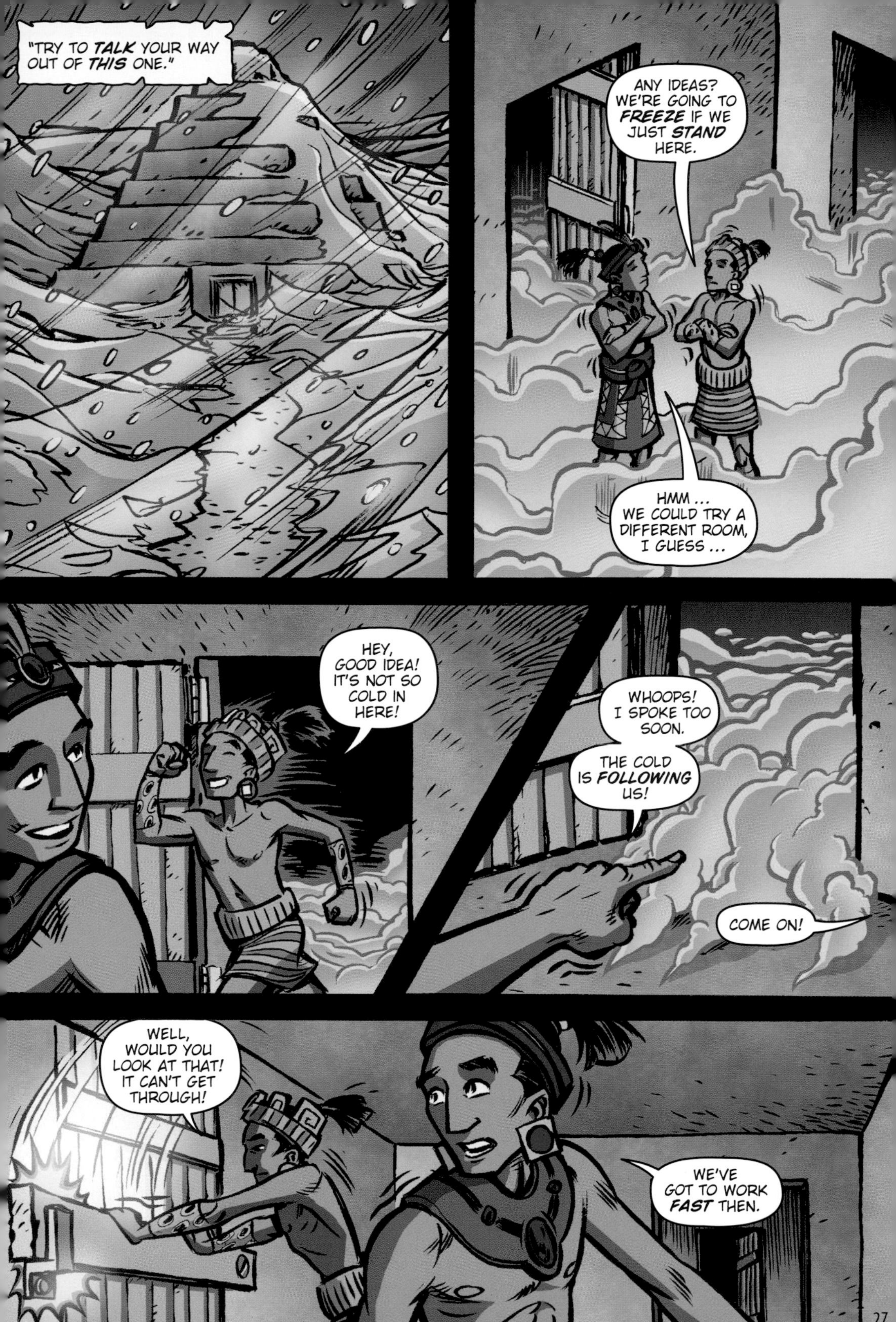

"TRY TO TALK YOUR WAY OUT OF THIS ONE."
ANY IDEAS? WE'RE GOING TO FREEZE IF WE JUST STAND HERE.
HMM ... WE COULD TRY A DIFFERENT ROOM, I GUESS ...
HEY, GOOD IDEA! IT'S NOT SO COLD IN HERE!
WHOOPS! I SPOKE TOO SOON.
THE COLD IS FOLLOWING US!
COME ON!
WELL, WOULD YOU LOOK AT THAT! IT CAN'T GET THROUGH!
WE'VE GOT TO WORK FAST THEN.

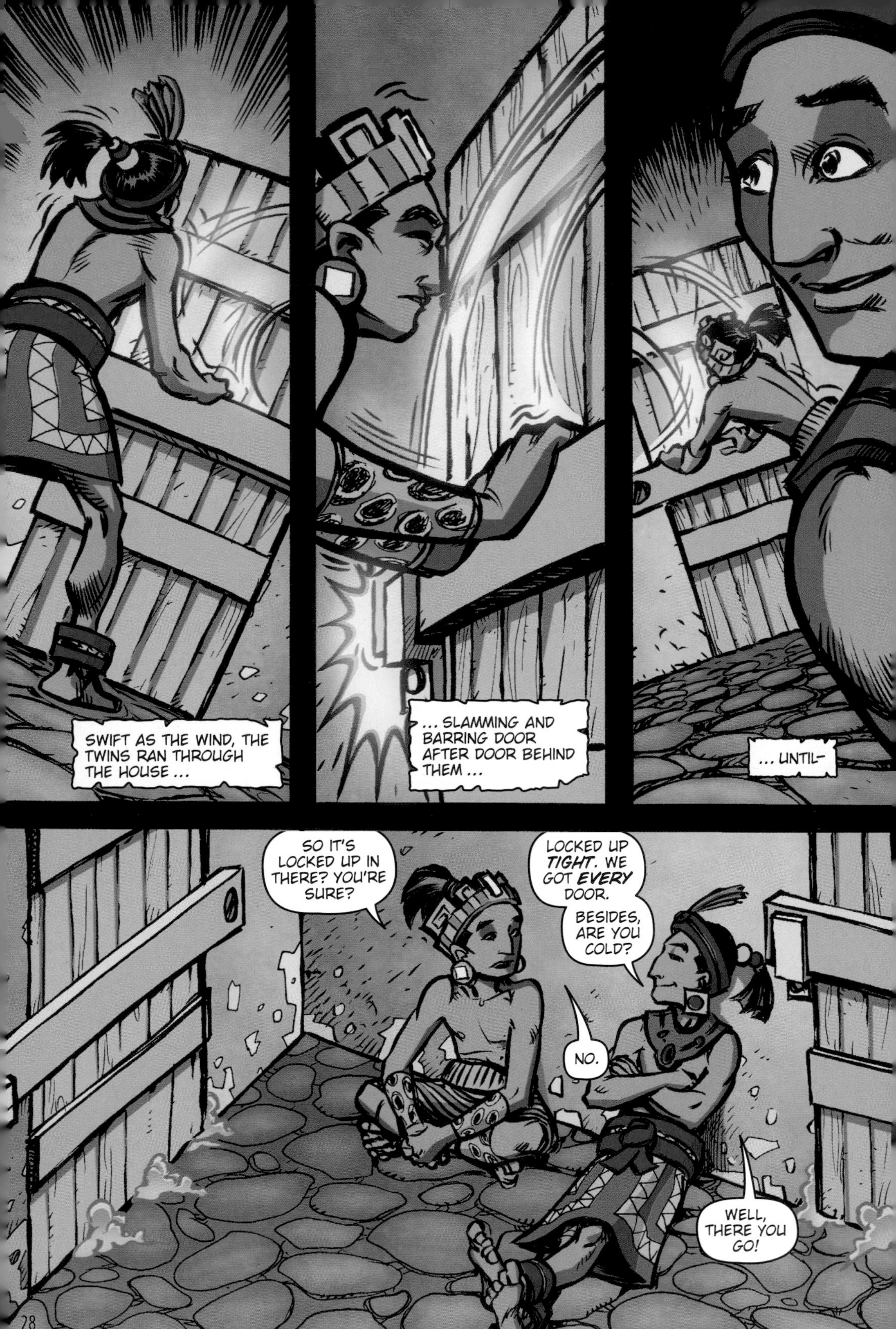
SWIFT AS THE WIND, THE TWINS RAN THROUGH THE HOUSE ...
... SLAMMING AND BARRING DOOR AFTER DOOR BEHIND THEM ...
... UNTIL-
SO IT'S LOCKED UP IN THERE? YOU'RE SURE?
LOCKED UP ***TIGHT***. WE GOT ***EVERY*** DOOR.
BESIDES, ARE YOU COLD?
NO.
WELL, THERE YOU GO!

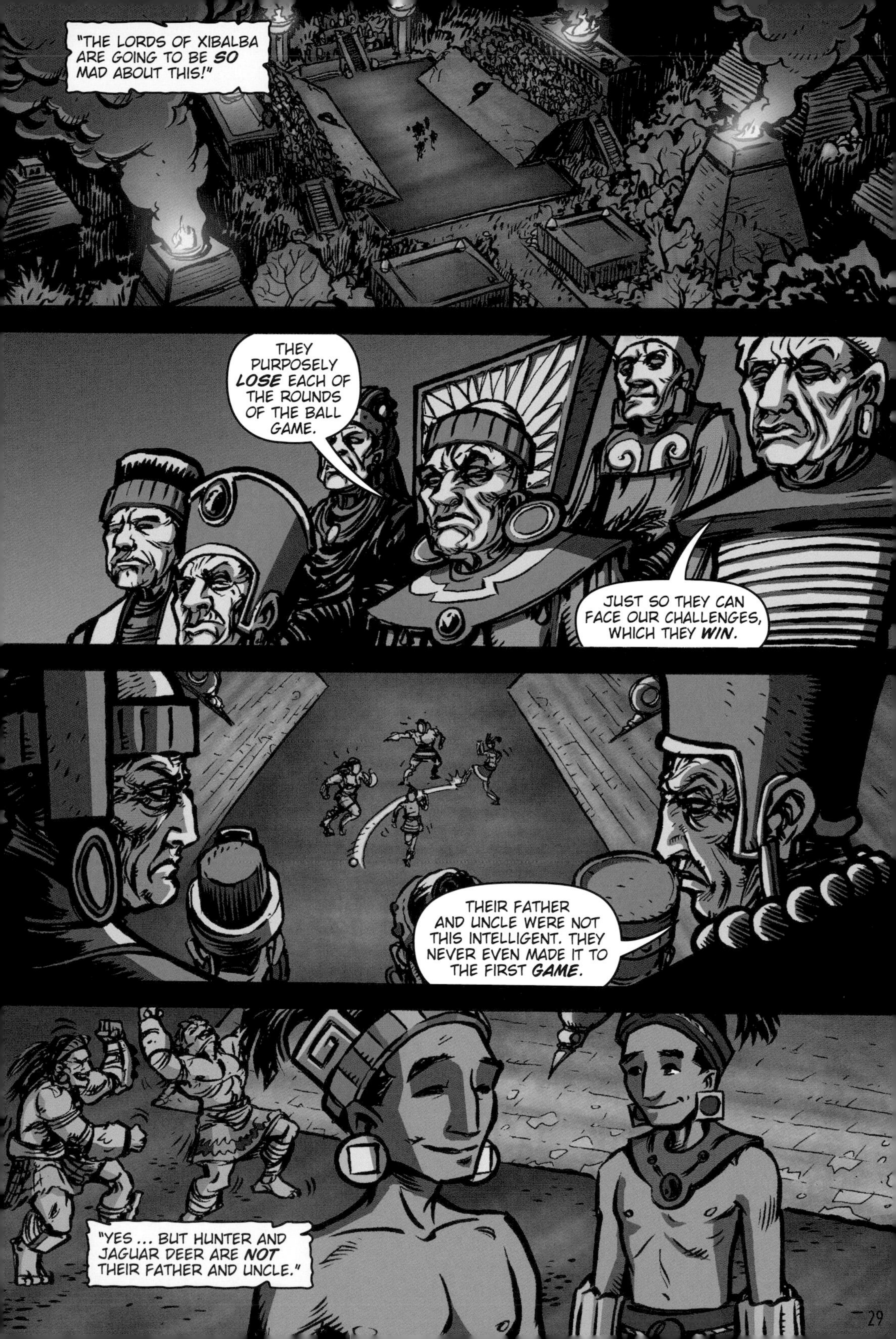
"THE LORDS OF XIBALBA ARE GOING TO BE *SO* MAD ABOUT THIS!"
THEY PURPOSELY *LOSE* EACH OF THE ROUNDS OF THE BALL GAME.
JUST SO THEY CAN FACE OUR CHALLENGES, WHICH THEY *WIN*.
THEIR FATHER AND UNCLE WERE NOT THIS INTELLIGENT. THEY NEVER EVEN MADE IT TO THE FIRST *GAME*.
"YES ... BUT HUNTER AND JAGUAR DEER ARE *NOT* THEIR FATHER AND UNCLE."

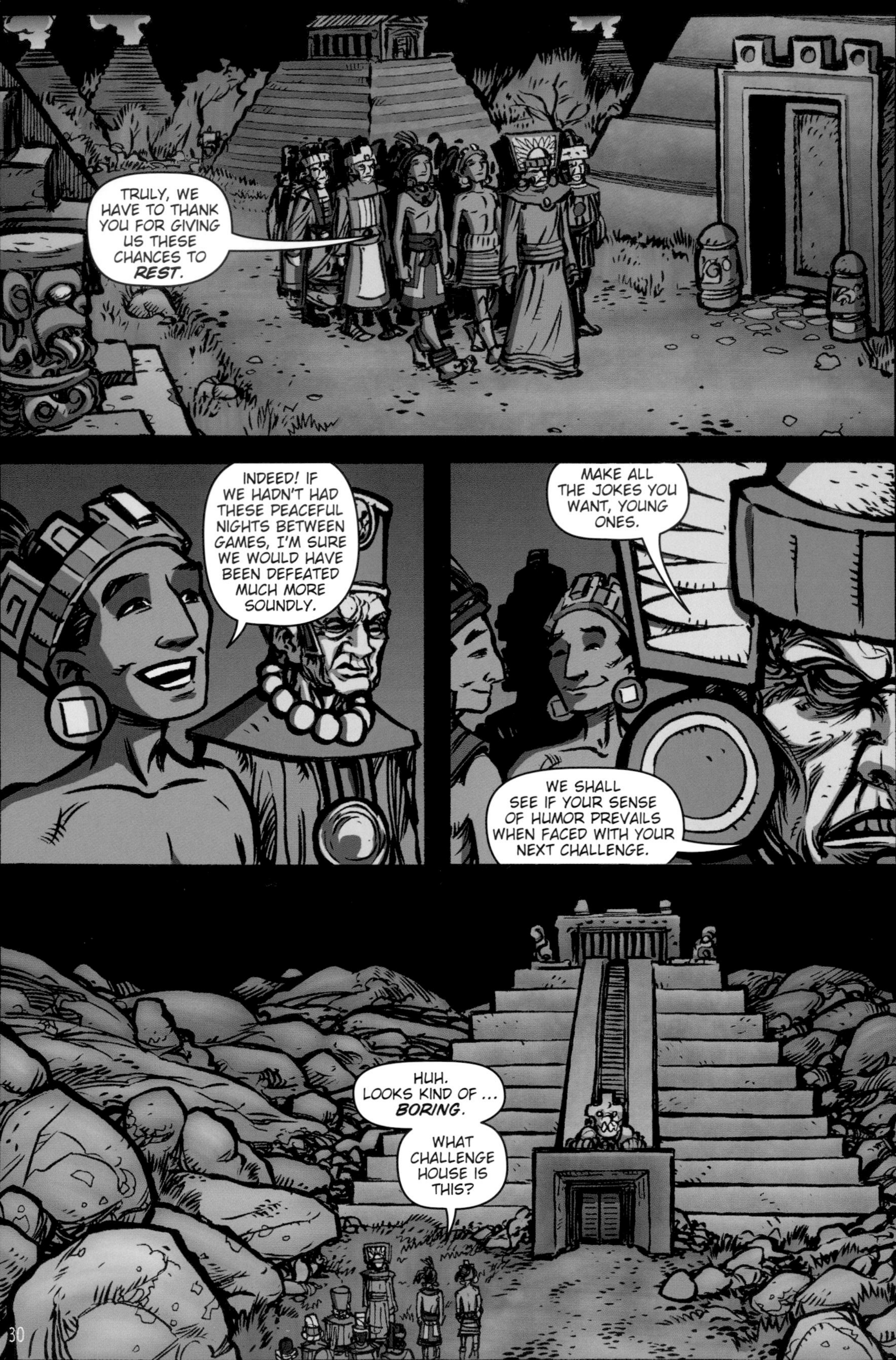
TRULY, WE HAVE TO THANK YOU FOR GIVING US THESE CHANCES TO *REST*.
INDEED! IF WE HADN'T HAD THESE PEACEFUL NIGHTS BETWEEN GAMES, I'M SURE WE WOULD HAVE BEEN DEFEATED MUCH MORE SOUNDLY.
MAKE ALL THE JOKES YOU WANT, YOUNG ONES.
WE SHALL SEE IF YOUR SENSE OF HUMOR PREVAILS WHEN FACED WITH YOUR NEXT CHALLENGE.
HUH. LOOKS KIND OF ... *BORING*.
WHAT CHALLENGE HOUSE IS THIS?

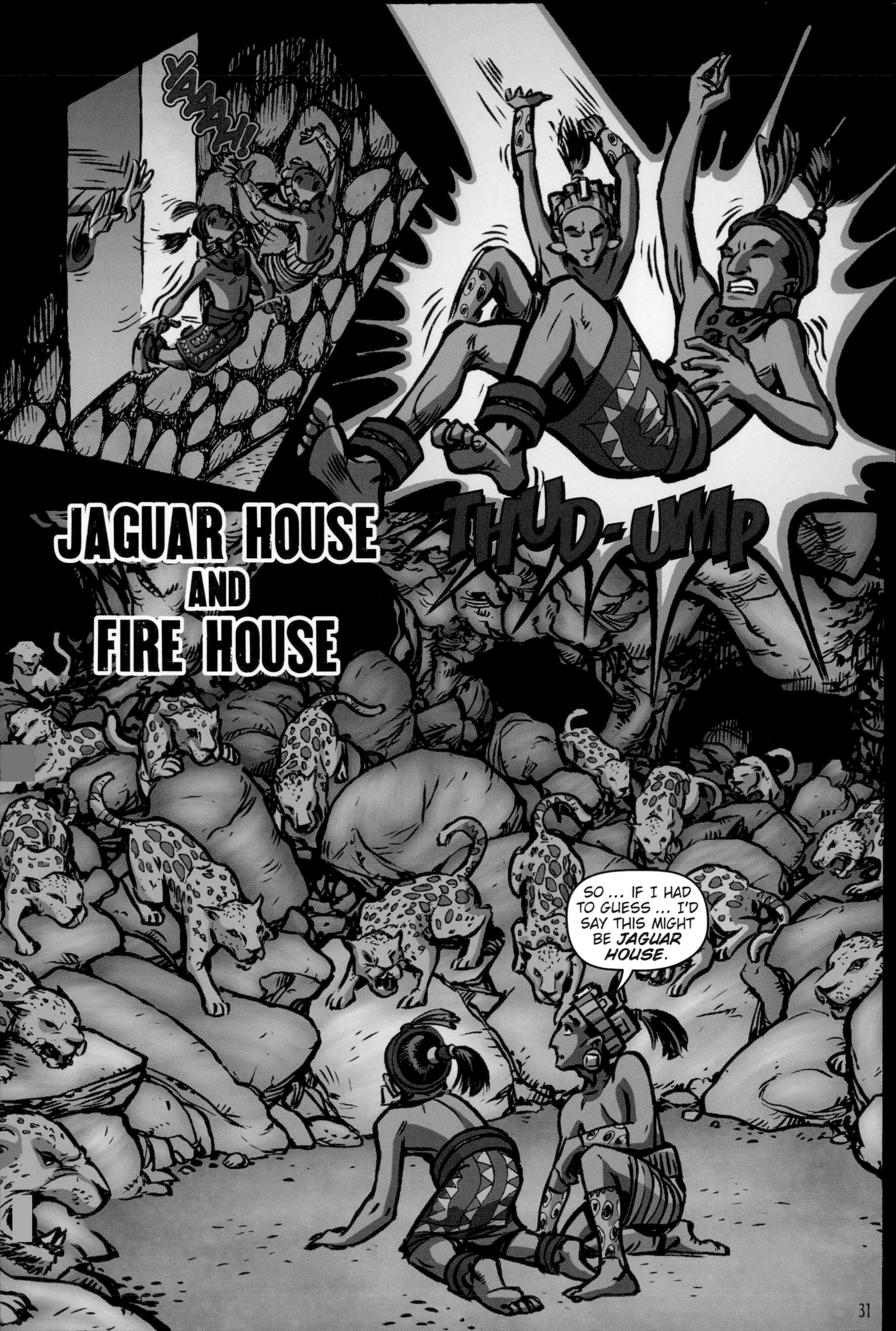
YAAAAH!
THUD-UMP
JAGUAR HOUSE AND FIRE HOUSE
SO ... IF I HAD TO GUESS ... I'D SAY THIS MIGHT BE JAGUAR HOUSE.

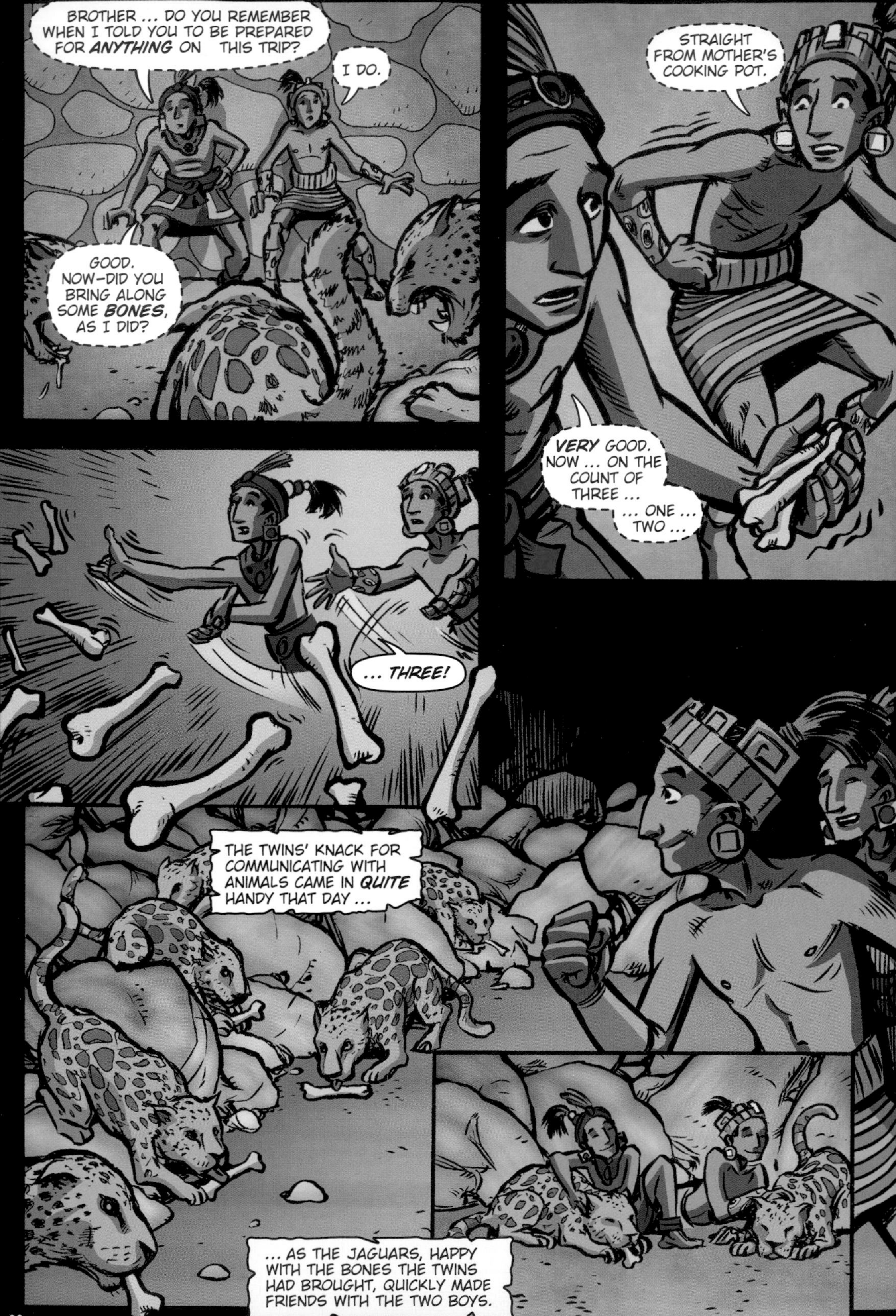

BROTHER ... DO YOU REMEMBER WHEN I TOLD YOU TO BE PREPARED FOR ANYTHING ON THIS TRIP?
I DO.
GOOD. NOW–DID YOU BRING ALONG SOME BONES, AS I DID?
STRAIGHT FROM MOTHER'S COOKING POT.
VERY GOOD. NOW ... ON THE COUNT OF THREE ...
... ONE ... TWO ...
... THREE!
THE TWINS' KNACK FOR COMMUNICATING WITH ANIMALS CAME IN QUITE HANDY THAT DAY ...
... AS THE JAGUARS, HAPPY WITH THE BONES THE TWINS HAD BROUGHT, QUICKLY MADE FRIENDS WITH THE TWO BOYS.

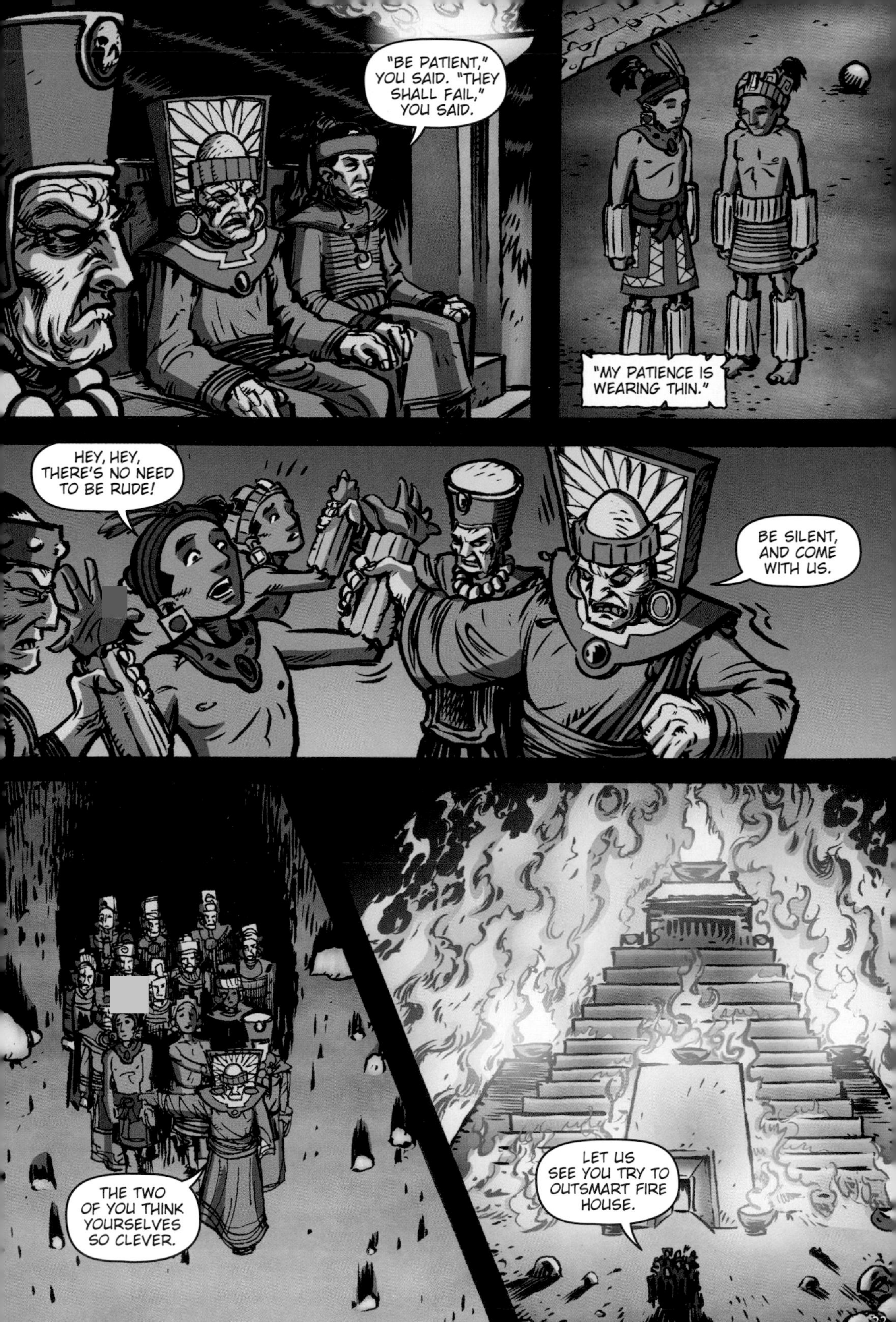
"BE PATIENT," YOU SAID. "THEY SHALL FAIL," YOU SAID.
"MY PATIENCE IS WEARING THIN."
HEY, HEY, THERE'S NO NEED TO BE RUDE!
BE SILENT, AND COME WITH US.
THE TWO OF YOU THINK YOURSELVES SO CLEVER.
LET US SEE YOU TRY TO OUTSMART FIRE HOUSE.

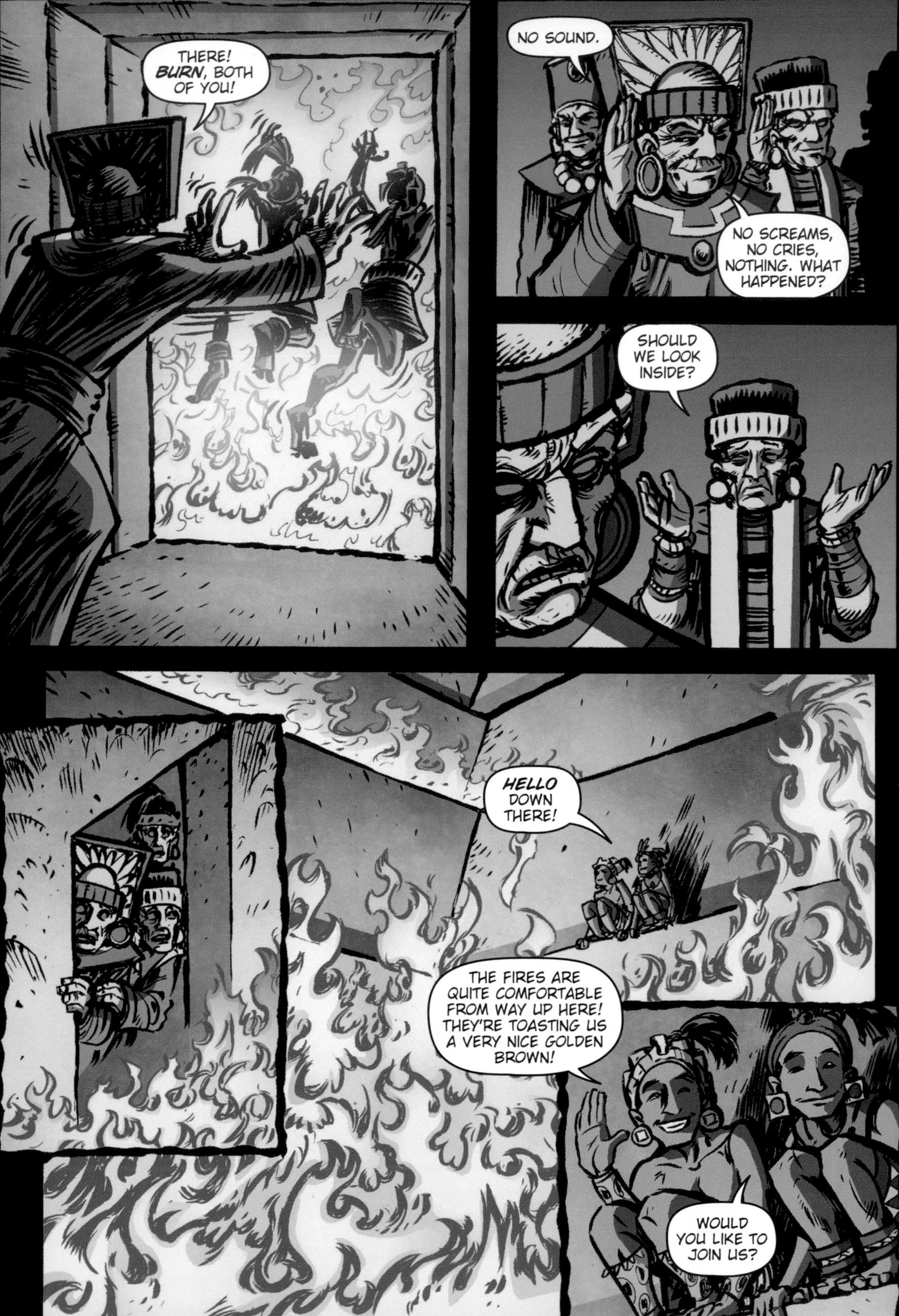
THERE! BURN, BOTH OF YOU!
NO SOUND.
NO SCREAMS, NO CRIES, NOTHING. WHAT HAPPENED?
SHOULD WE LOOK INSIDE?
HELLO DOWN THERE!
THE FIRES ARE QUITE COMFORTABLE FROM WAY UP HERE! THEY'RE TOASTING US A VERY NICE GOLDEN BROWN!
WOULD YOU LIKE TO JOIN US?

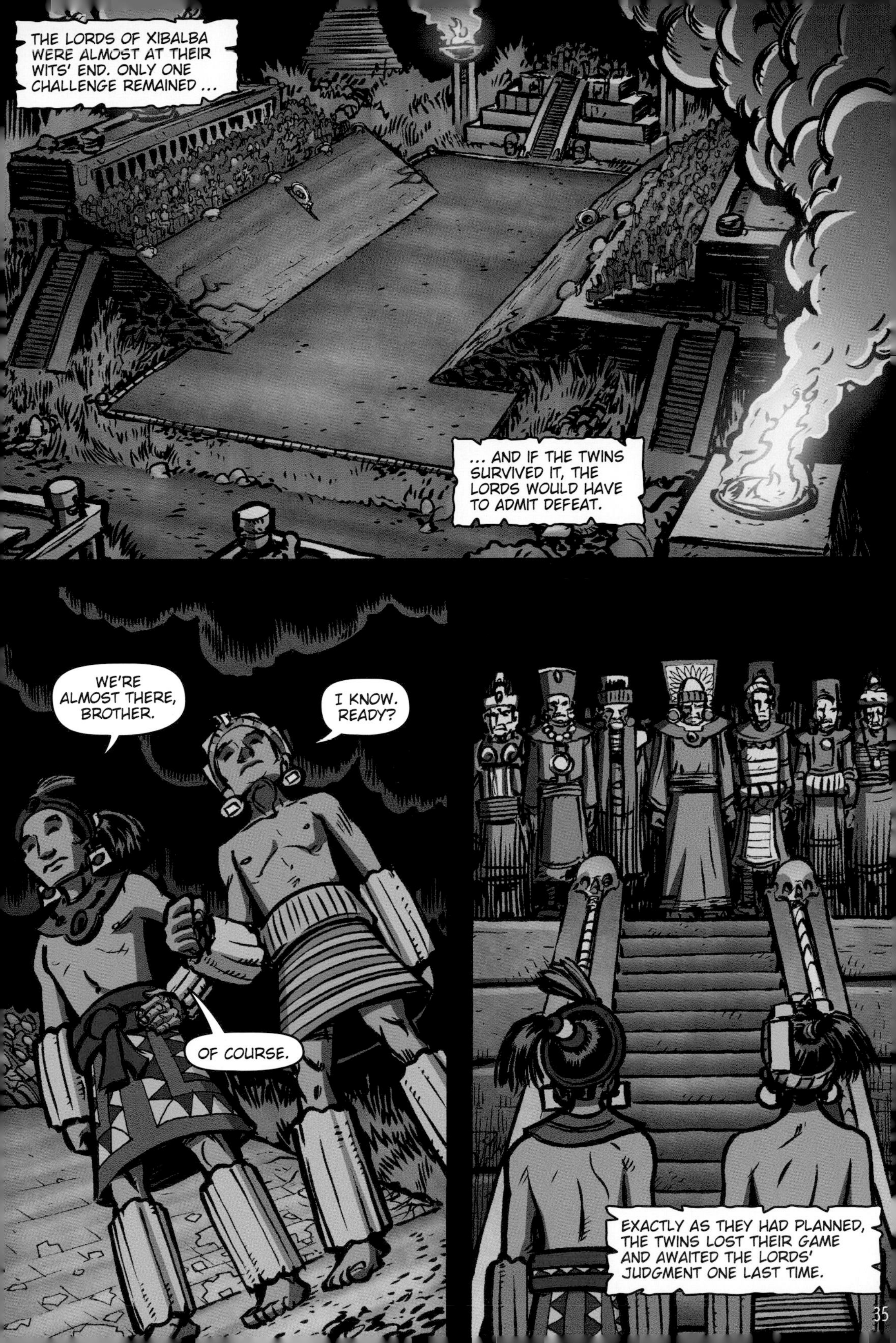
THE LORDS OF XIBALBA WERE ALMOST AT THEIR WITS' END. ONLY ONE CHALLENGE REMAINED ...
... AND IF THE TWINS SURVIVED IT, THE LORDS WOULD HAVE TO ADMIT DEFEAT.
WE'RE ALMOST THERE, BROTHER.
I KNOW. READY?
OF COURSE.
EXACTLY AS THEY HAD PLANNED, THE TWINS LOST THEIR GAME AND AWAITED THE LORDS' JUDGMENT ONE LAST TIME.

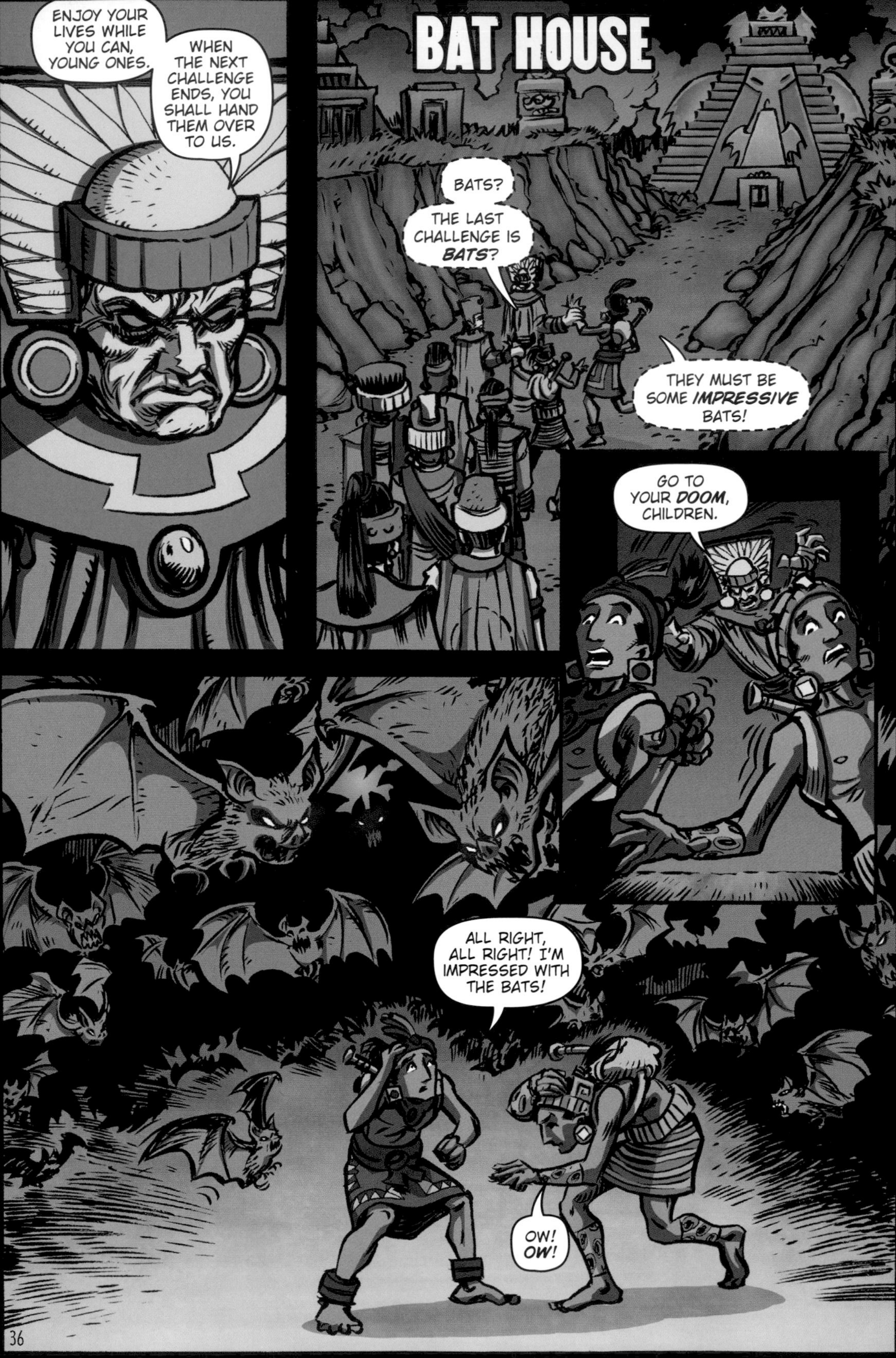
ENJOY YOUR LIVES WHILE YOU CAN, YOUNG ONES.
WHEN THE NEXT CHALLENGE ENDS, YOU SHALL HAND THEM OVER TO US.
BAT HOUSE
BATS?
THE LAST CHALLENGE IS BATS?
THEY MUST BE SOME IMPRESSIVE BATS!
GO TO YOUR DOOM, CHILDREN.
ALL RIGHT, ALL RIGHT! I'M IMPRESSED WITH THE BATS!
OW! OW!

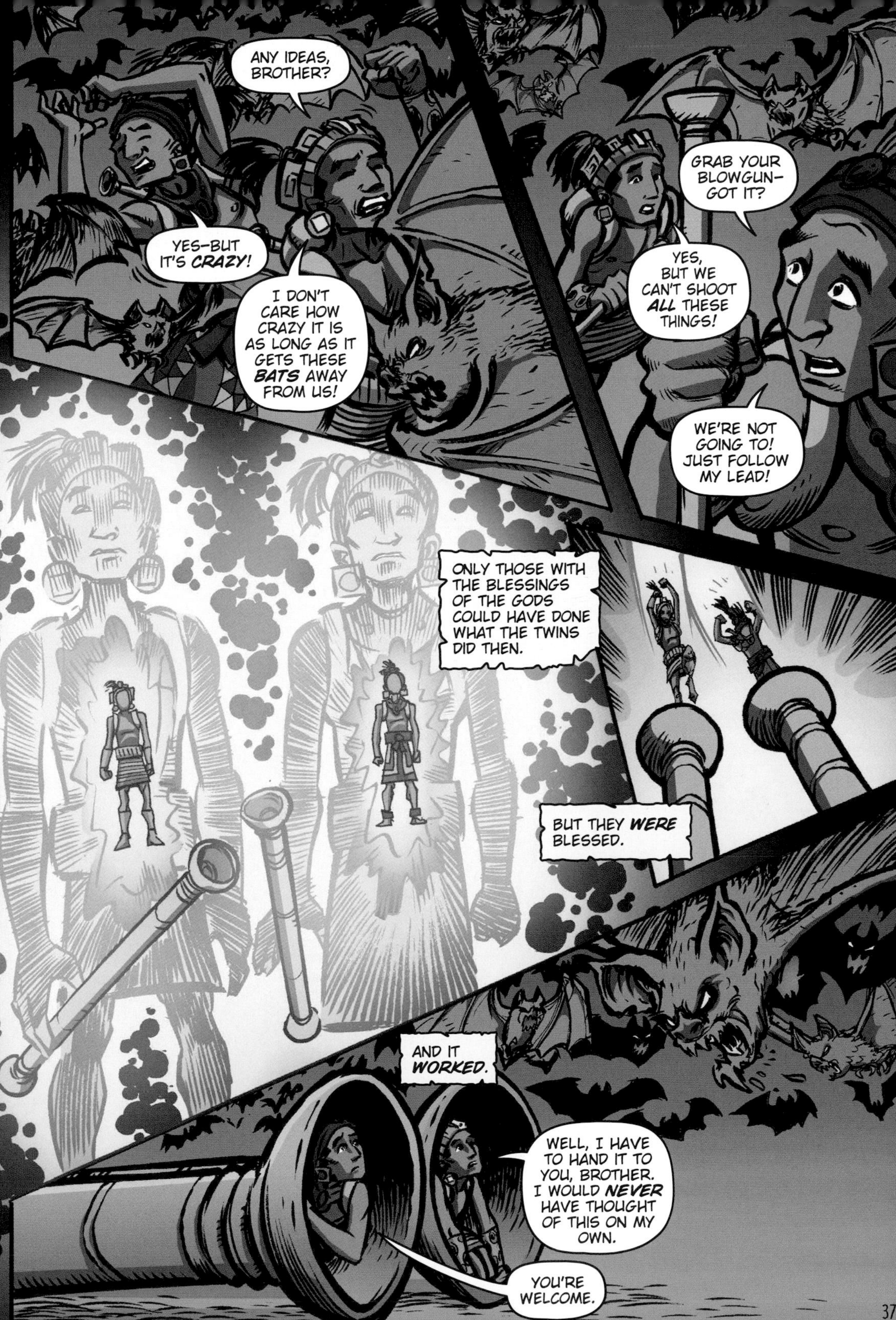
ANY IDEAS, BROTHER?
YES–BUT IT'S *CRAZY*!
I DON'T CARE HOW CRAZY IT IS AS LONG AS IT GETS THESE *BATS* AWAY FROM US!
GRAB YOUR BLOWGUN–GOT IT?
YES, BUT WE CAN'T SHOOT *ALL* THESE THINGS!
WE'RE NOT GOING TO! JUST FOLLOW MY LEAD!
ONLY THOSE WITH THE BLESSINGS OF THE GODS COULD HAVE DONE WHAT THE TWINS DID THEN.
BUT THEY *WERE* BLESSED.
AND IT *WORKED*.
WELL, I HAVE TO HAND IT TO YOU, BROTHER. I WOULD *NEVER* HAVE THOUGHT OF THIS ON MY OWN.
YOU'RE WELCOME.

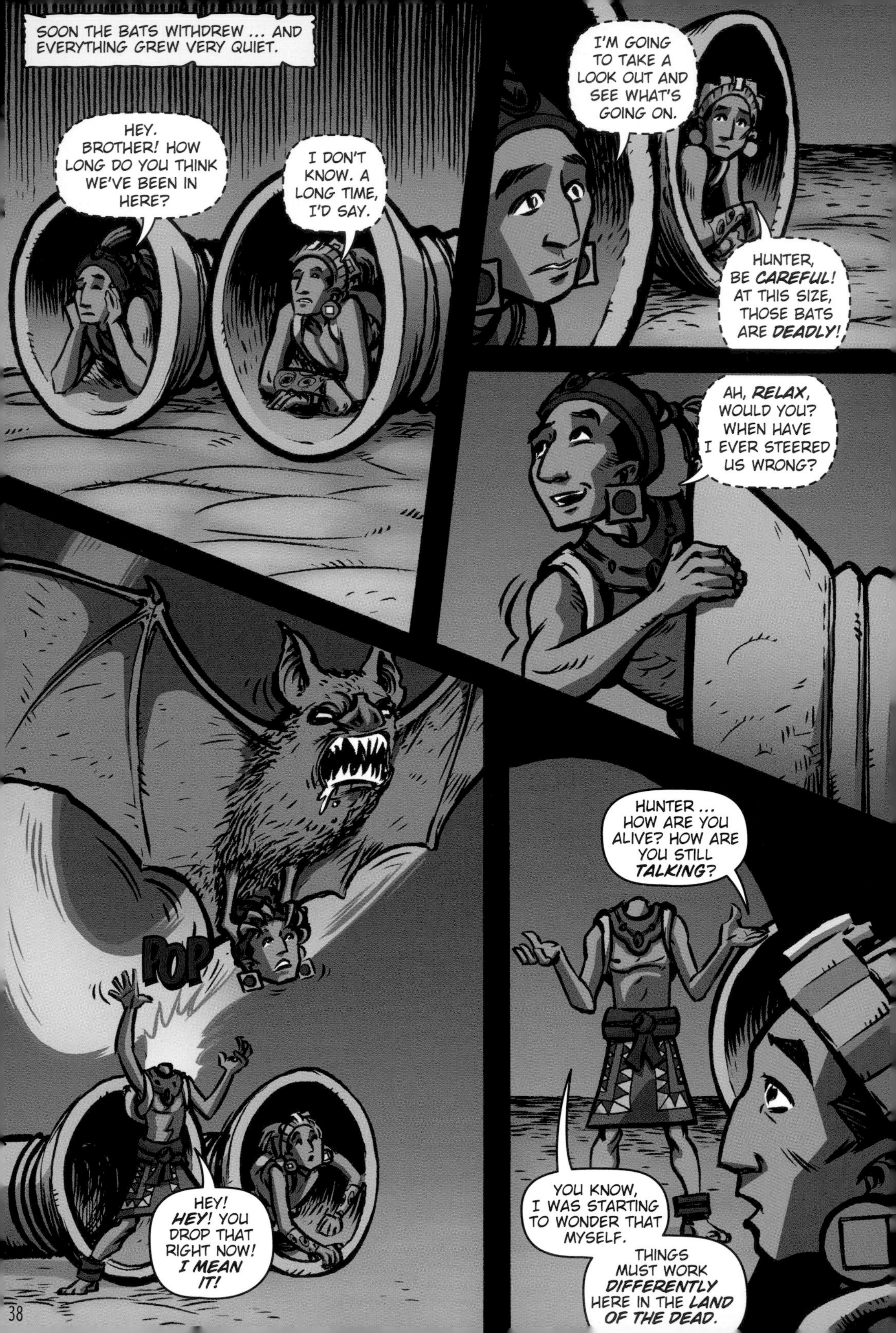

SOON THE BATS WITHDREW ... AND EVERYTHING GREW VERY QUIET.
HEY. BROTHER! HOW LONG DO YOU THINK WE'VE BEEN IN HERE?
I DON'T KNOW. A LONG TIME, I'D SAY.
I'M GOING TO TAKE A LOOK OUT AND SEE WHAT'S GOING ON.
HUNTER, BE *CAREFUL*! AT THIS SIZE, THOSE BATS ARE *DEADLY*!
AH, *RELAX*, WOULD YOU? WHEN HAVE I EVER STEERED US WRONG?
POP
HEY! *HEY!* YOU DROP THAT RIGHT NOW! *I MEAN IT!*
HUNTER ... HOW ARE YOU ALIVE? HOW ARE YOU STILL *TALKING*?
YOU KNOW, I WAS STARTING TO WONDER THAT MYSELF.
THINGS MUST WORK *DIFFERENTLY* HERE IN THE *LAND OF THE DEAD*.

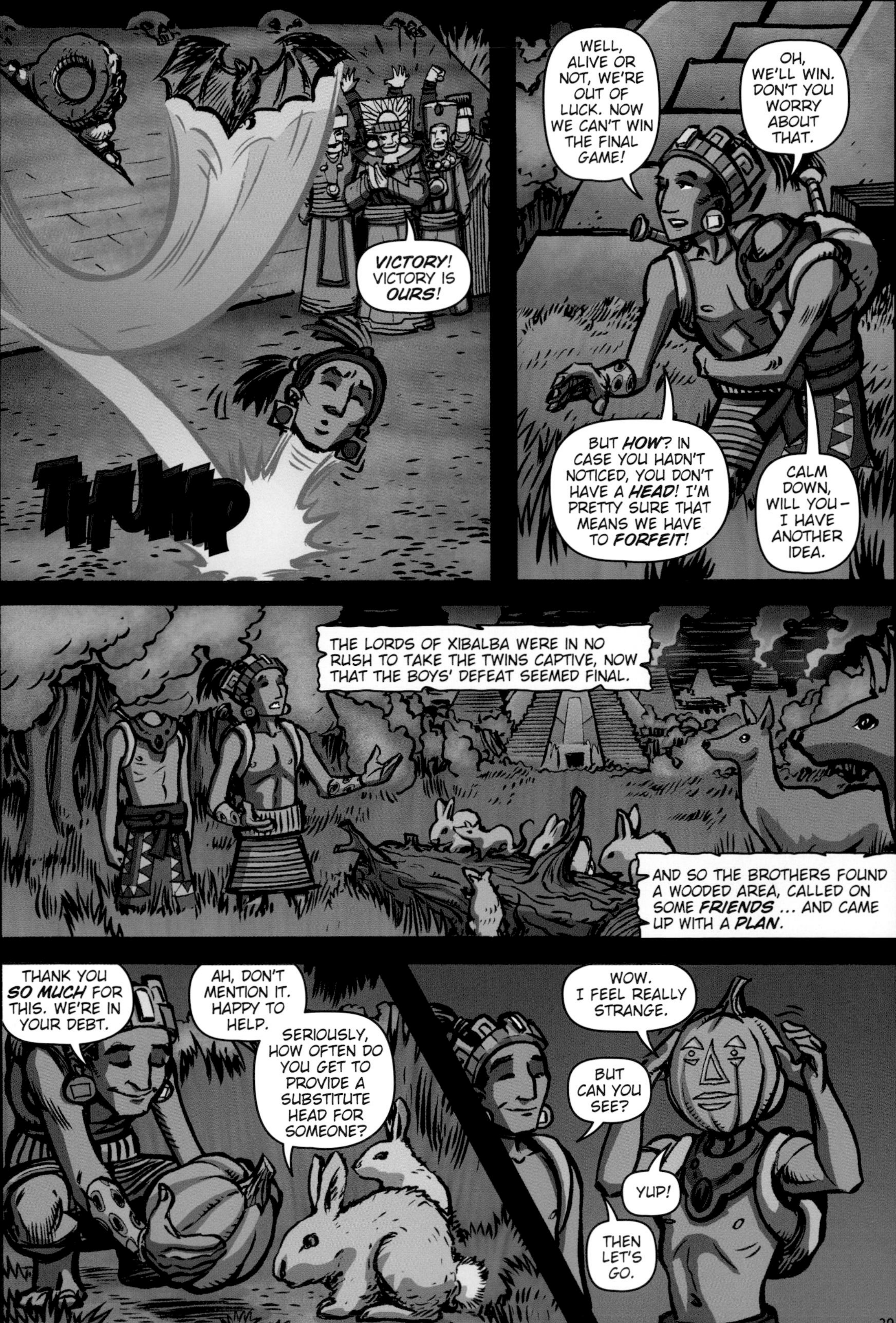
VICTORY! VICTORY IS OURS!
THUMP
WELL, ALIVE OR NOT, WE'RE OUT OF LUCK. NOW WE CAN'T WIN THE FINAL GAME!
OH, WE'LL WIN. DON'T YOU WORRY ABOUT THAT.
BUT HOW? IN CASE YOU HADN'T NOTICED, YOU DON'T HAVE A HEAD! I'M PRETTY SURE THAT MEANS WE HAVE TO FORFEIT!
CALM DOWN, WILL YOU– I HAVE ANOTHER IDEA.
THE LORDS OF XIBALBA WERE IN NO RUSH TO TAKE THE TWINS CAPTIVE, NOW THAT THE BOYS' DEFEAT SEEMED FINAL.
AND SO THE BROTHERS FOUND A WOODED AREA, CALLED ON SOME FRIENDS ... AND CAME UP WITH A PLAN.
THANK YOU SO MUCH FOR THIS. WE'RE IN YOUR DEBT.
AH, DON'T MENTION IT. HAPPY TO HELP.
SERIOUSLY, HOW OFTEN DO YOU GET TO PROVIDE A SUBSTITUTE HEAD FOR SOMEONE?
WOW. I FEEL REALLY STRANGE.
BUT CAN YOU SEE?
YUP!
THEN LET'S GO.

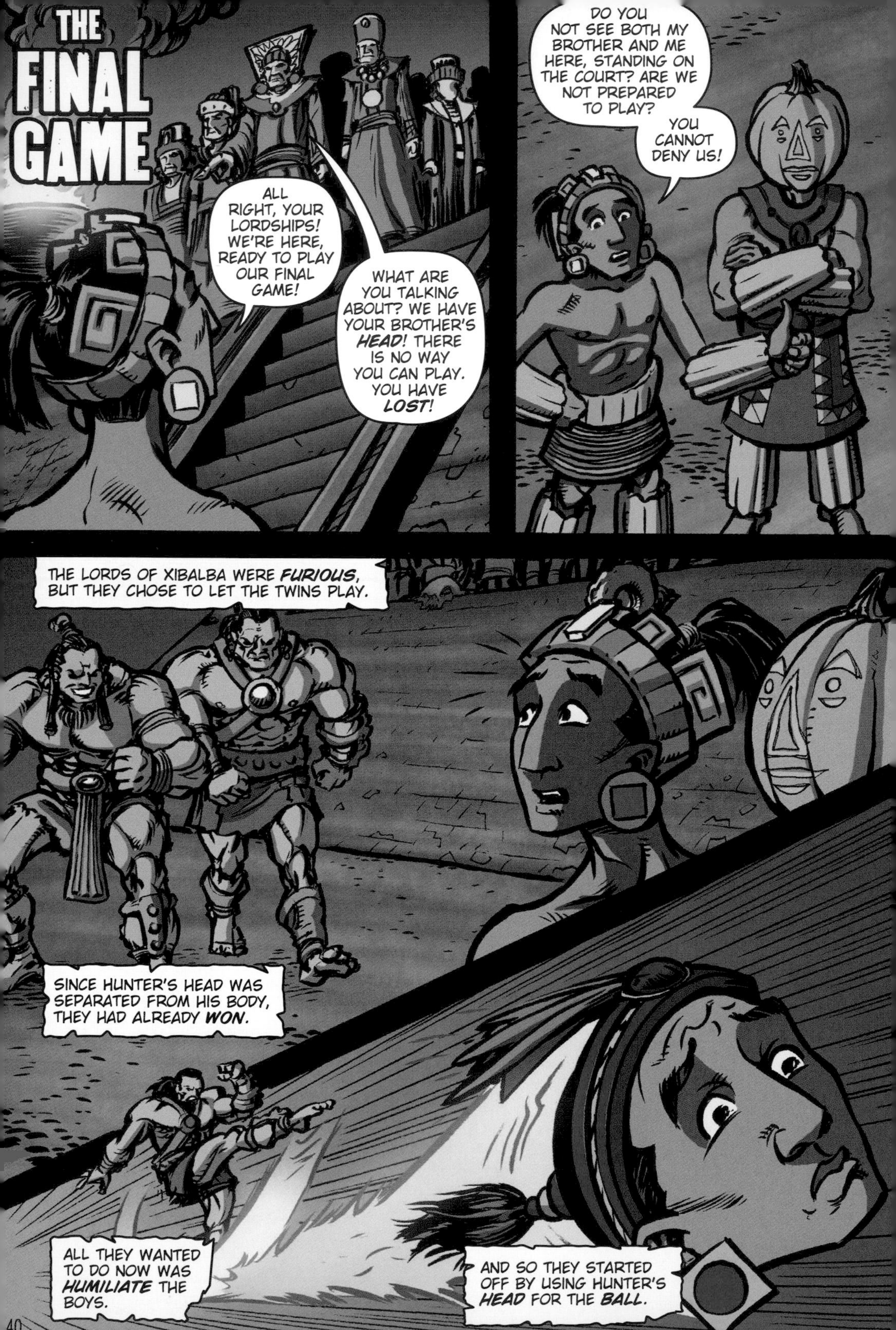
THE FINAL GAME
ALL RIGHT, YOUR LORDSHIPS! WE'RE HERE, READY TO PLAY OUR FINAL GAME!
WHAT ARE YOU TALKING ABOUT? WE HAVE YOUR BROTHER'S HEAD! THERE IS NO WAY YOU CAN PLAY. YOU HAVE LOST!
DO YOU NOT SEE BOTH MY BROTHER AND ME HERE, STANDING ON THE COURT? ARE WE NOT PREPARED TO PLAY?
YOU CANNOT DENY US!
THE LORDS OF XIBALBA WERE FURIOUS, BUT THEY CHOSE TO LET THE TWINS PLAY.
SINCE HUNTER'S HEAD WAS SEPARATED FROM HIS BODY, THEY HAD ALREADY WON.
ALL THEY WANTED TO DO NOW WAS HUMILIATE THE BOYS.
AND SO THEY STARTED OFF BY USING HUNTER'S HEAD FOR THE BALL.

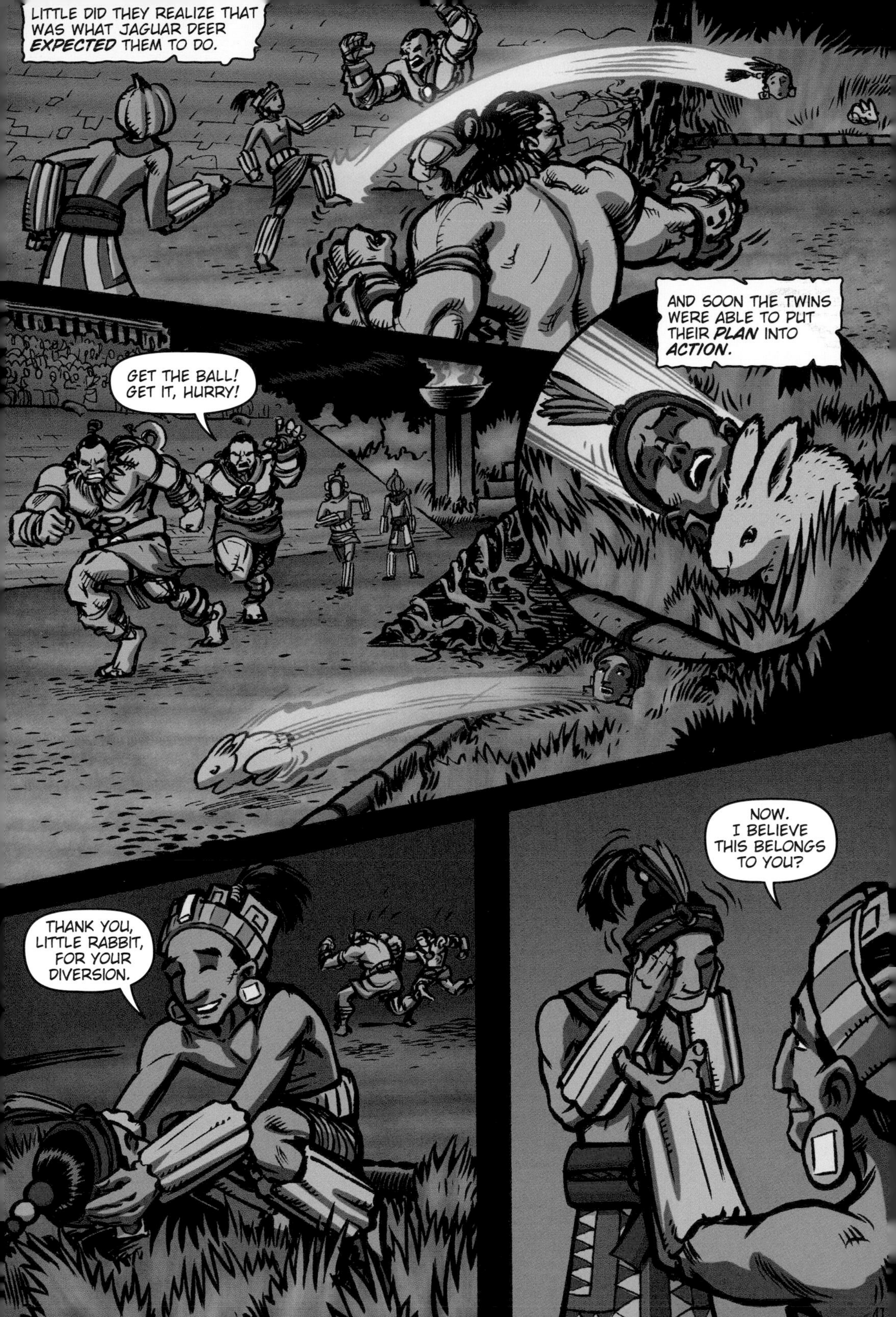

LITTLE DID THEY REALIZE THAT WAS WHAT JAGUAR DEER EXPECTED THEM TO DO.
AND SOON THE TWINS WERE ABLE TO PUT THEIR PLAN INTO ACTION.
GET THE BALL! GET IT, HURRY!
THANK YOU, LITTLE RABBIT, FOR YOUR DIVERSION.
NOW. I BELIEVE THIS BELONGS TO YOU?

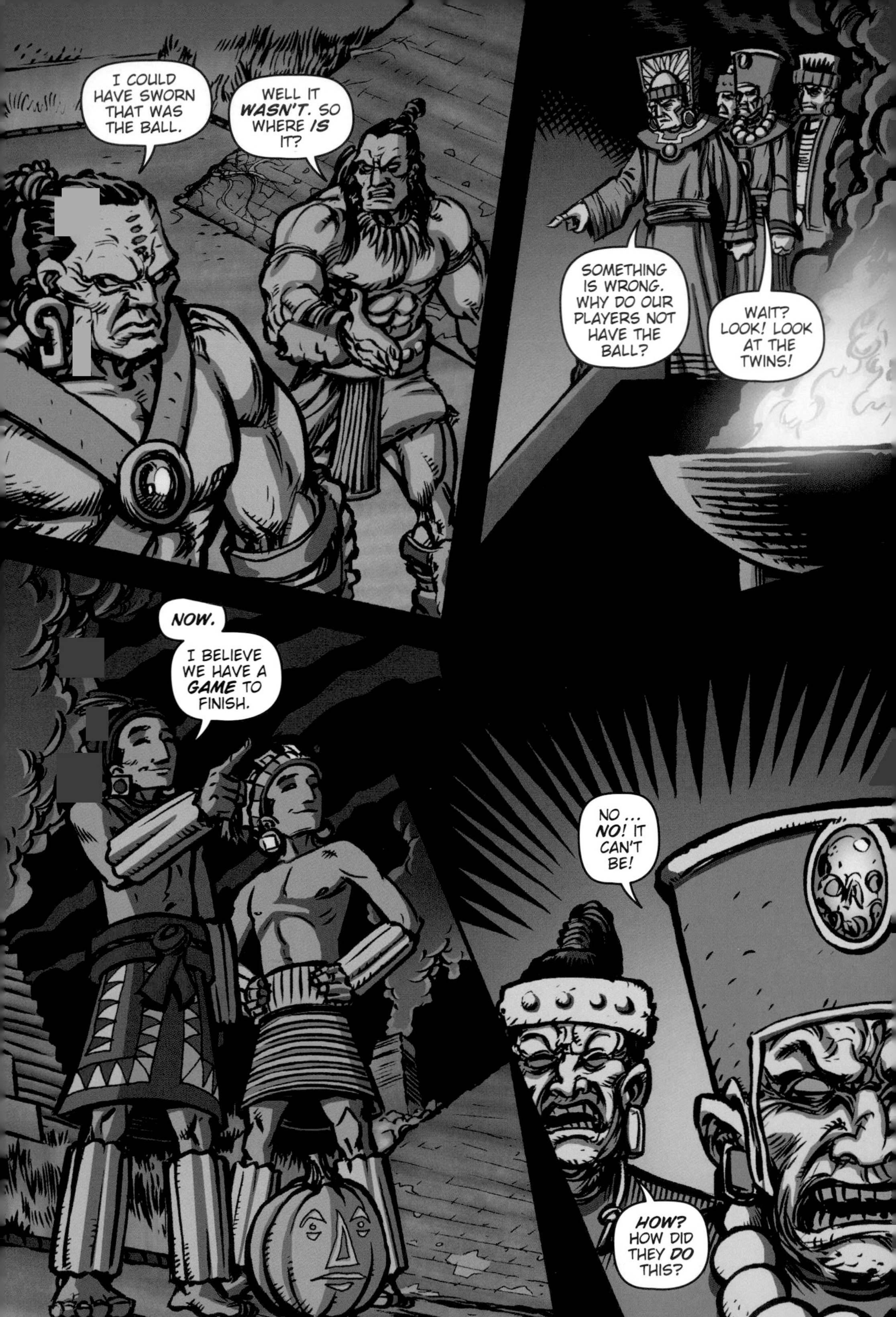
I COULD HAVE SWORN THAT WAS THE BALL.
WELL IT ***WASN'T***. SO WHERE ***IS*** IT?
SOMETHING IS WRONG. WHY DO OUR PLAYERS NOT HAVE THE BALL?
WAIT? LOOK! LOOK AT THE TWINS!
NOW.
I BELIEVE WE HAVE A ***GAME*** TO FINISH.
NO ... ***NO!*** IT CAN'T BE!
HOW? HOW DID THEY ***DO*** THIS?

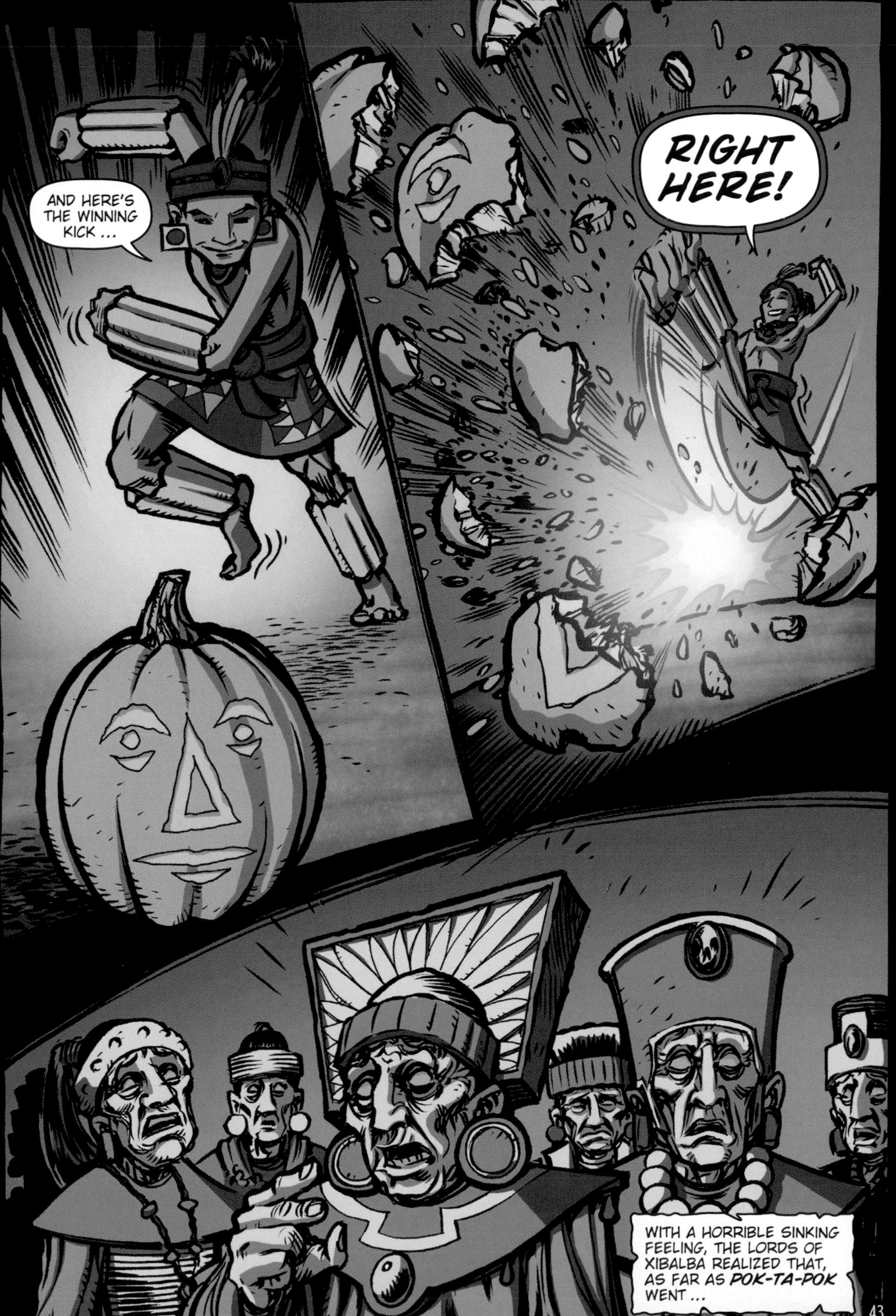
AND HERE'S THE WINNING KICK ...
RIGHT HERE!
WITH A HORRIBLE SINKING FEELING, THE LORDS OF XIBALBA REALIZED THAT, AS FAR AS *POK-TA-POK* WENT ...

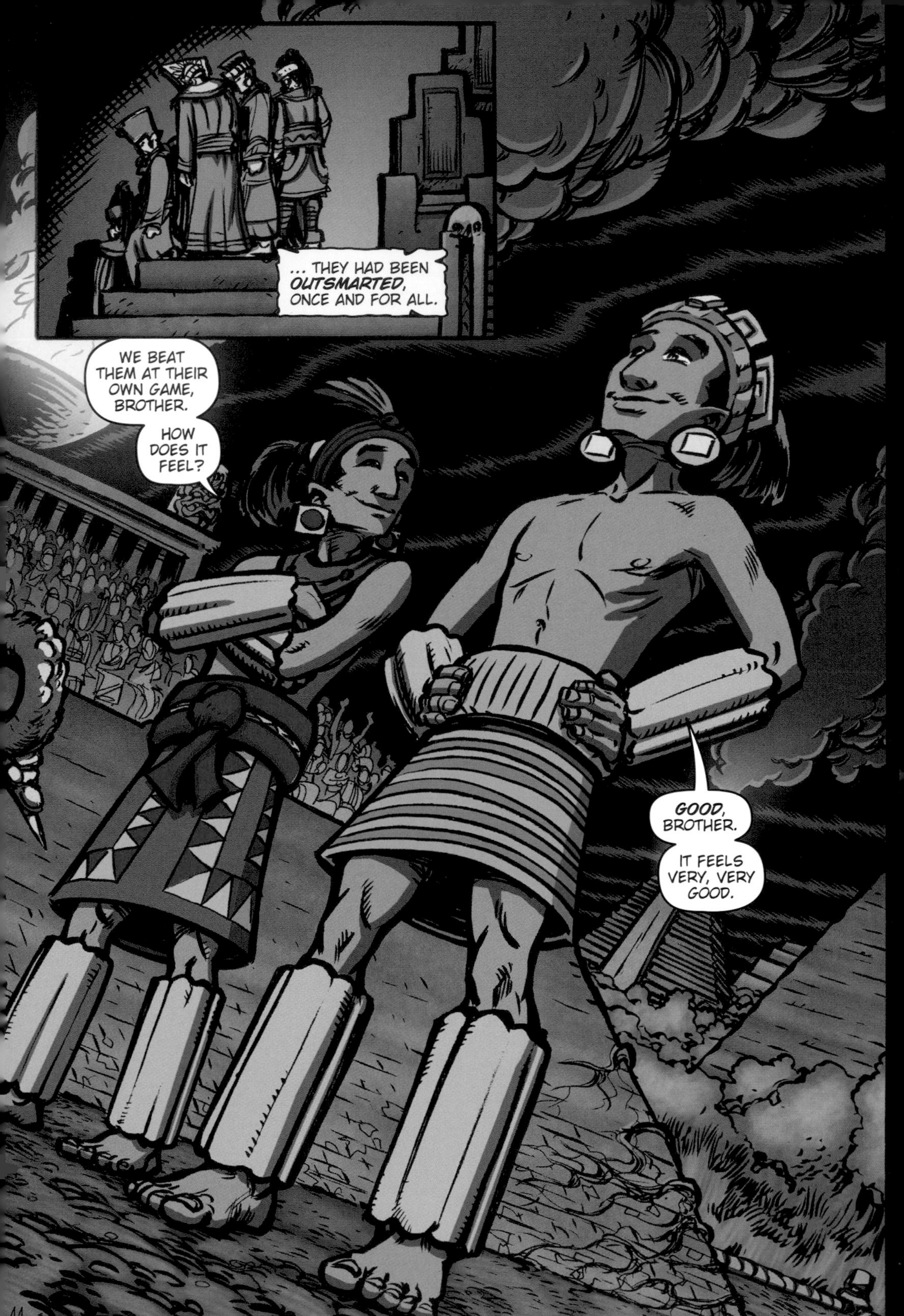
... THEY HAD BEEN **OUTSMARTED**, ONCE AND FOR ALL.
WE BEAT THEM AT THEIR OWN GAME, BROTHER.
HOW DOES IT FEEL?
GOOD, BROTHER.
IT FEELS VERY, VERY GOOD.

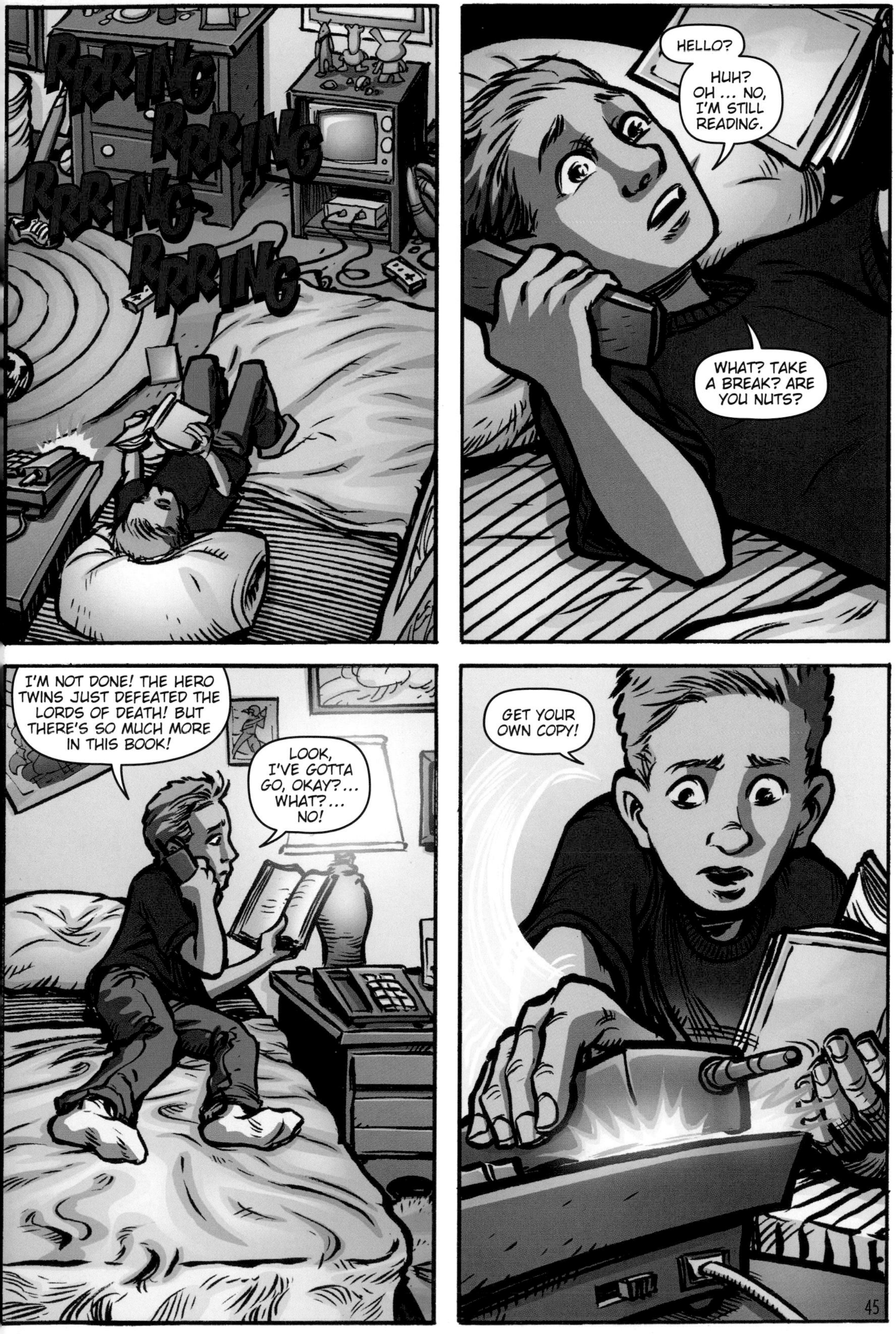
RRRING RRRING RRRING RRRING
HELLO?
HUH? OH ... NO, I'M STILL READING.
WHAT? TAKE A BREAK? ARE YOU NUTS?
I'M NOT DONE! THE HERO TWINS JUST DEFEATED THE LORDS OF DEATH! BUT THERE'S SO MUCH MORE IN THIS BOOK!
LOOK, I'VE GOTTA GO, OKAY?... WHAT?... NO!
GET YOUR OWN COPY!

GLOSSARY AND PRONUNCIATION GUIDE

HUNAHPU (hoo-nah-*poo*): the hero twin also known as Hunter

POK-TA-POK (pohk-ta-*pohk*): the ancient Mayan ball game

POPOL VUH (*poh*-pohl *voo*, or poh-*pohl woo*): an ancient Mayan text that includes the story of the Hero Twins as well as many other tales

QUICHÉ MAYA (kee-*chay mah*-yuh): a Mayan ethnic group, creators of the *Popol Vuh*

XBALANQUE (sh-bah-lahn-*kay*): the Hero Twin also known as Jaguar Deer

XIBALBA (shee-bahl-*bah*): the underworld of Mayan folklore

XIBALBAN (shee-*bahl*-bahn): someone who lives in Xibalba

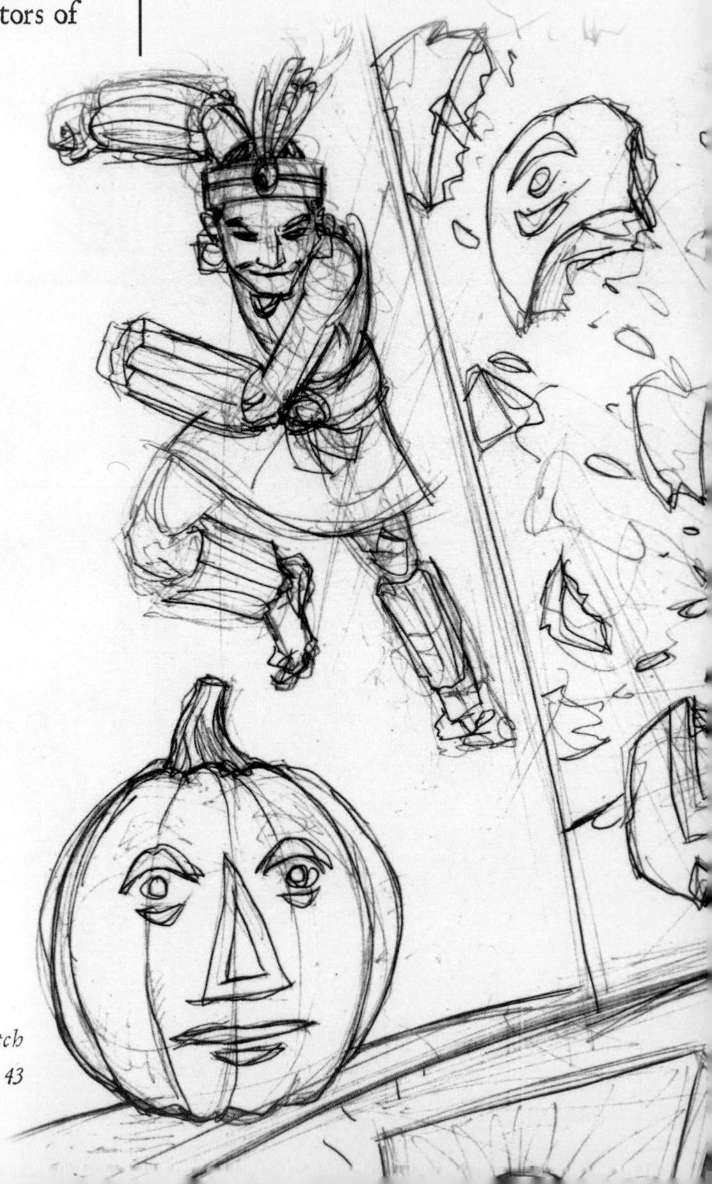

original pencil sketch from page 43

FURTHER READING AND WEBSITES

Bierhorst, John. *The Monkey's Haircut and Other Stories Told by the Maya*. New York: HarperCollins Publishers, 1986. "The Monkey's Haircut" is one of twenty-two fascinating Mayan stories in this collection compiled by one of the world's foremost experts on folktales of the Americas.

Clarke, Barry, and Elizabeth Baquedano. *Aztec, Inca, and Maya*. New York: DK Publishing, 2005. Learn more about the ancient Maya—as well as the Aztec and Inca—in this photo- and fact-filled volume from the Eyewitness Books series.

Day, Nancy. *Your Travel Guide to Ancient Mayan Civilization*. Minneapolis: Twenty-First Century Books, 2001. Day prepares readers for a trip back to ancient Mayan civilization, including which places to visit, how to get around, what to wear, and how to fit in with the locals.

Mayan Kids.com
http://www.mayankids.com/
This educational website features kid-friendly information about the Mayan people and Mayan civilization, including details about the Mayan ball game often called pok-ta-pok or pok-a-tok.

Perl, Lila. *The Ancient Maya*. New York: Franklin Watts, 2005. Learn more about the ancient Maya from this volume in the People of the Ancient World series.

CREATING *THE HERO TWINS: AGAINST THE LORDS OF DEATH*

Author Dan Jolley consulted several translations of the *Popol Vuh* to create this book. To create authentic costuming and setting, artist David Witt reviewed numerous books exploring Mayan history, art, and architecture. Finally, Mesoamerican folklore expert John Bierhorst reviewed the story and the artwork to ensure its authenticity and respect for the Mayan tradition.

INDEX

ABOUT THE AUTHOR AND THE ARTIST

DAN JOLLEY began his writing career in the early nineties. His limited series *Obergeist* was voted Best Horror Comic of 2001 by *Wizard* magazine, and his DC Comics project *JSA: The Unholy Three* received an Eisner Award nomination (the comics industry's highest honor) for Best Limited Series of 2003. May of 2007 saw the debut of Jolley's first novel series, an original young-adult sci-fi espionage story called *Alex Unlimited*, published by a joint venture of TokyoPop and HarperCollins. He's also scripting the manga project *Warriors: The Lost Warrior*, based on the novel series by Erin Hunter, as well as writing the novelization of the motion picture *Iron Man*. Jolley lives in Cary, North Carolina, where he's on the design team of Icarus Studios' post-apocalyptic MMORPG, *Fallen Earth*. Jolley spends more time playing video games than he probably should.

DAVID WITT is a busy all-purpose illustrator. In addition to his work for Graphic Universe's Graphic Myths and Legends series (which includes *Isis and Osiris: To the Ends of the Earth*) and Twisted Journeys series (*Captured by Pirates*), he creates flyers, posters, screenprints, comics, T-shirt designs, logos, and all variety of illustrations and paintings for the world to enjoy. Witt lives in Minneapolis, Minnesota.